**PAGODA** Books

2B
Fourth Edition
Generations

# SLE

SPEAKING · LISTENING · EXPRESSION

**Copyright** © 2012, 2008, 2001, 1997 PAGODA Academy, Inc.

All rights reserved. No part of this publication may be reproduced, stored in a retrieval system, or transmitted, in any form, or by any means, electronic, mechanical, photocopying, recording or otherwise, without the prior written permission of the copyright holder and the publisher.

**Published by** Wit&Wisdom

Wit&Wisdom is the professional language publishing company of the **PAGODA** Education Group.
19F, PAGODA Tower, 419, Gangnam-daero,
Seocho-gu, Seoul, 06614, Rep. of KOREA
www.pagodabook.com

**Imprint** | PAGODA Books

**First published 2012**
**Eighth impression 2018**
**Printed in the Republic of Korea**

**ISBN** 978-89-6281-454-5 (13740)

**Publisher** | Ru-Da Go
**Writers** | Judson Wright, Lee Robinson, Kristin Quackenbush
**Editor** | Paul Adams
**Advisor** | Ruda Go
**Illustrator** | Dae Ho Kim

**Acknowledgements**
Sang Hee Kang, Song Rim Park, Hana Sakuragi, Stephen Willetts, Ian Windsor, and Gemma Young for their support
Nathan Benzschawel, Christina Bromberg, Patrick Farrell, Christopher Jack, Donald Nairn, and Tiara Smith for trialing and feedback
Rich Debourke, Jess Kroll, Tiara Smith, and Gemma Young for voice recording.

A defective book may be exchanged at the store where you purchased it.

# To Our Students

The SLE program is a conversation program for adult and young adult students who want to improve their English in an enjoyable, effective, and authentic way. The book allows students to use English in a variety of contexts with an emphasis on different useful functions. Our goal is to improve your confidence in your speaking, listening, reading, and writing ability while improving your vocabulary and grammar skills. We will help you to understand not only the "How" but the "Why" of English usage.

The SLE Level 2 textbook series is meant for students with a very good understanding of the basics of English. The material in this book focuses on building students' ability to perform basic functions and use essential structures.

# Contents SLE 2B

To Our Students | 3
Format of the Book | 6
Goals for the Course | 7
Meet the Thompson Family | 8

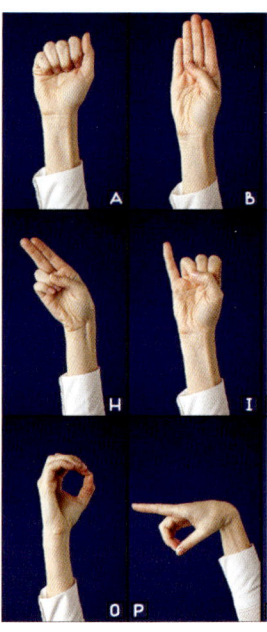

### UNIT 1
**All the Time in the World**
Hobbies & Free Time
▶ 11

LESSON 1 | 12
LESSON 2 | 16

### UNIT 2
**The Numbers Game**
Vague & Precise
▶ 27

LESSON 1 | 28
LESSON 2 | 34

### UNIT 3
**Communication Breakdown**
Rumors & Misunderstandings
▶ 45

LESSON 1 | 46
LESSON 2 | 52

### UNIT 4
**Better Safe Than Sorry**
Social & Global Problems
▶ 63

LESSON 1 | 64
LESSON 2 | 70

### UNIT 5
**You Don't Say**
Nonverbal Communication & Defining Characteristics
▶ 81

LESSON 1 | 82
LESSON 2 | 88

Listening Dialogues | 182
Glossary | 190

### UNIT 6
**Coulda, Woulda, Shoulda**
Past Speculations & Regrets
▶ 101

LESSON 1 | 102
LESSON 2 | 110

### UNIT 7
**Make Yourself at Home**
Culture & Nation Building
▶ 119

LESSON 1 | 120
LESSON 2 | 126

### UNIT 8
**The Grass is Always Greener**
Pros, Cons, & Contrasts
▶ 135

LESSON 1 | 136
LESSON 2 | 144

### UNIT 9
**The Future is Now**
Future Speculations & Technology
▶ 153

LESSON 1 | 154
LESSON 2 | 162

### UNIT 10
**Looking Back**
Bringing It All Together
▶ 171

LESSON 1 | 172

# Format of the Book:

### Overall Format >
There are ten units in this textbook, each with its own focus. In each unit there are two individual lessons. The focus of the lesson is either grammatical or topical. Each unit consists of the following elements:

### Warm Up >
The warm up for each lesson has its own purpose. The lesson one warm up is used as an opportunity to start thinking about the topic and includes functional language such as idioms, collocations, and tongue twisters that relate to the topic as a whole. The lesson two warm up is used as a quick review of the language used in the first lesson and a bridge to the second lesson.

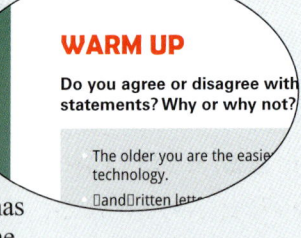

### Listening >
Each listening follows the story of the Thompson family and relates to the unit topic and language points used in that unit. Each listening requires the student to make predictions based on illustrations and use communicative language to discuss what they have heard.

### Language Point >
Language points occur at the start of any activity where a specific grammar or function point is used in that activity and needs to be explained to the student.

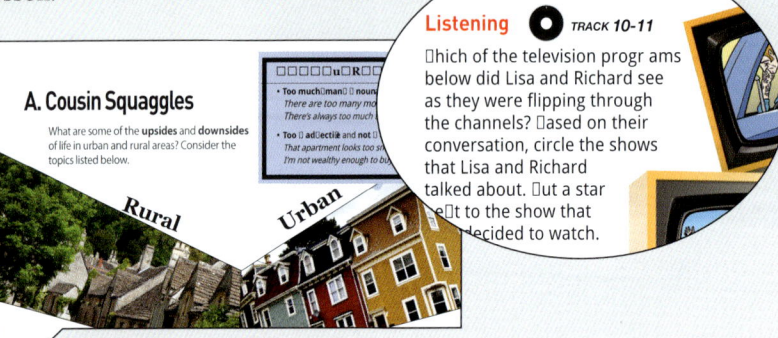

### Activities >
Each lesson consists of a structured activity, a communicative activity, and a task based activity. All units include a "Bonus activity" that can add to the lesson.

### Discussion Questions >
Each lesson has a short series of discussion questions that relate to the topic and encourage the use of asking follow up questions.

### Boxes > 
Several boxes are found throughout the text and have different functions:

• **Recycle Box**
Reminds the student of language points they have used previously in SLE.

• **Third Wheel**
Gives a suggestion of how students can perform an activity with an extra student.

• **Do You Know?**
Explains the reason why language is used in a specific way.

• **Do You Remember?**
Reminds students of vocabulary from a previous lesson.

• **Tip**
Gives a tip on how the student can acquire the language more easily.

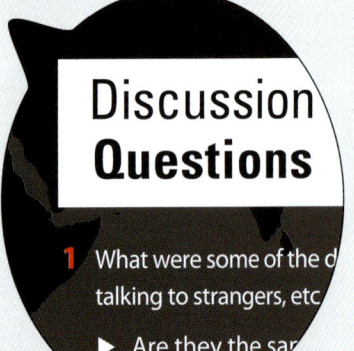

### Segue Activity >
The segue activity consists of a reading that relates to the topic of the listening, discussion questions which check the comprehension of the reading, and a short writing task on the topic.

# Goals for the Course:

## 1
### You should be able to use the following grammatical structures:

**a** Used to and didn't use to

**b** Go + verb + ing and Go + to

**c** Prepositions of time

**d** Past speculation using modal verbs

**e** Contrast using even though and although

**f** Relative pronouns in adjective clauses

**g** Imperatives

**h** Future speculation using modal verbs

## 2
### You should be able to perform the following functions:

**a** Understanding when and how to describe in vague and precise ways

**b** Checking and confirming information

**c** Resolving misunderstandings

**d** Expressing levels of importance with modal verbs

**e** Interpreting and using nonverbal communication

**f** Expressing degrees of certainty in the past tense and future tense

**g** Talking about regrets

**h** Discussing living situations

**i** Making contrasts

- Making recommendations and suggestions
- Giving advice
- Comparisons

### Did You Know?
**"Get in" vs. "Get on"**

These two phrasal verbs are very similar! When talking about travel, "get on" is generally used for vehicles in which you can stand, and "get in" is used for vehicles in which you must sit.

**3rd wheel**
If you are the third member in this activity, interrupt the speakers politely, offer your own greeting, and join the conversation.

**Tip** What's a follow-up question? Asking a follow-up question is an important part of keeping a conversation going. By asking follow-up questions you are showing interest in the conversation.

**objectives:**
- Use indirect questions
- Listen to a story about scams

### Do You Remember?
creativity, patience, dedication, honesty, social skills, organization, judgement, passion

* see glossary for definitions

### Need to Know:

- **to be fired**
Lucas **was fired** from his job because he stole money from the safe.

- **to be laid off**
Because of budget cuts, thirty employees **were laid off** last week.

- **to retire**
My parents **retired** when they were 60 years old.

- **to quit**
She **quit** her job because the salary was too low.

- **to get promoted**
When Fred **got promoted**, he received a higher salary.

# Meet the Thompson Family
## Several of the activities will follow their lives and daily routines.

### Jack Thompson

**Age:** 22
**Blood type:** A
**Job:** Senior at University

Jack is a friendly, relaxed young man, though many people think he is very lazy. He enjoys drinking with his friends and listening to his favorite band: the Crimson Kings. He will graduate from university soon and is starting to look for a new job. But not very hard.

### Susan Thompson

**Age:** 42
**Blood type:** B
**Job:** Owns a small catering business

Susan is a logical, smart, and independent woman. She loves reading non-fiction, especially biographies. In her free time, Susan enjoys relaxing with an old movie and a large cup of tea. She recently found out that she is pregnant with her third child!

### Baby Jane

### Charles Thompson

**Age:** 67
**Blood type:** O
**Job:** Retired

Richard's Father. Charles is an adventurous old man with the heart of a child. He doesn't always consider the consequences of his actions. When he was younger, he joined the military and traveled the world. He enjoys hiking and fishing.

# Richard Thompson

**Age:** 45
**Blood type:** A
**Job:** Marketing

Richard is a motivated, hard-working, and creative man. He enjoys spending time with his family. He is an excellent cook. He also reads lots of different newspapers. He is very good at his job, and he recently received a new promotion.

# Martha Thompson

**Age:** 65
**Blood type:** A
**Job:** Retired

Richard's Mother. Martha is a kind and quirky old woman, though sometimes she is a little forgetful. She writes poetry and secretly loves watching reality television. She is very concerned about eating healthy food.

# Lisa Thompson

**Age:** 19
**Blood type:** AB
**Job:** Freshman at University

Lisa is an ambitious and outgoing young woman, though her ambition sometimes means she gets easily stressed. She graduated high school last year and this is her first year of university. She loves going to the park on sunny days and shopping on rainy days.

# Mr. Squiggles

**Age:** 3
**Job:** Cat

Mr. Squiggles is the playful family cat. He enjoys eating, scratching furniture, taking naps in Lisa's lap, and chasing Jack around the house. Sometimes, he likes to take Susan's things and hide them under the couch.

*Humm... Are You Ready To Meet Them?*

# 01
# All the Time in the World
Hobbies and Free Time

**Objectives:**
/ Discuss current and past personal information
/ Listen to a story about a childhood nickname

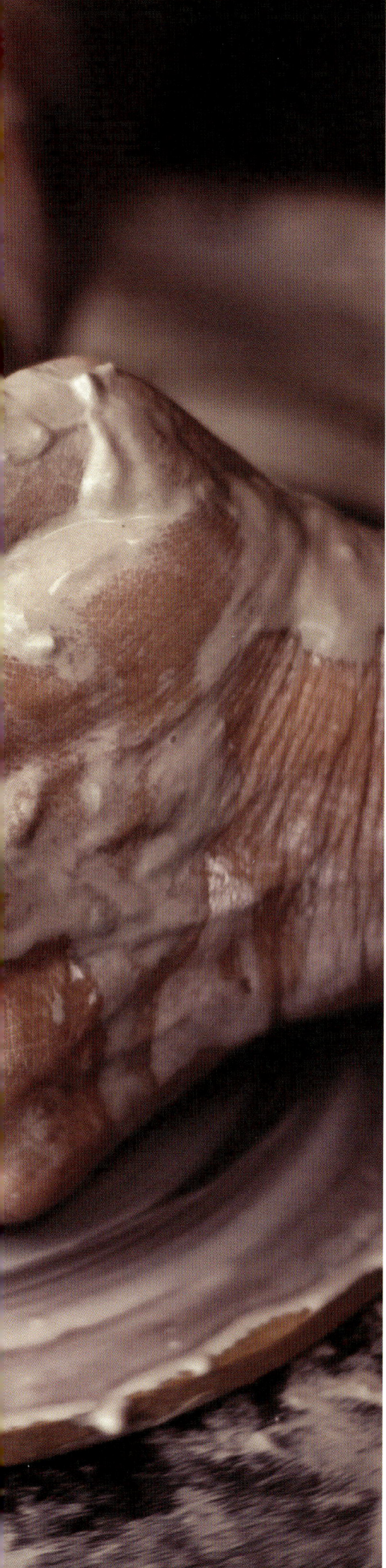

## WARM UP

A. What did you do last weekend?

- What did you have to do?
- What did you do for fun?

B. How much free time do you have in a typical week?

- Do you wish you had more/less free time?

### PHRASAL VERBS

- **Hang out**
  I like to *hang out* with my friends during the weekend.
- **Go out**
  I'm not planning to *go out* this weekend because I'm tired.

### IDIOMS

- **Pass time**
  I'm looking for a way to *pass time* between work and class.
- **Swamped**
  I'm always *swamped* at work, so I never really have any free time.

### COLLOCATIONS

- **Keep busy**
  All my hobbies have been *keeping me busy* lately.
- **Occupy time**
  Since you just broke up with your boyfriend, you should find a way to *occupy your time*.

# LESSON 1

## A. The "Why" Game

**Tip**
What's a follow up question? Asking a follow up question is an important part of keeping a conversation going. By asking follow up questions you are showing interest in the conversation.

**PART 1** ● Get to know your partner by discussing the questions below. For each question given here, ask three follow up questions using the words provided.

**Student A:** *What do you usually do in your free time?*
**Student B:** *Well, I really like to knit.*
**Student A:** *Wow! When did you start knitting?*
**Student B:** *I only started to knit about two weeks ago.*
**Student A:** *How did you learn to knit?*
**Student B:** *My grandmother taught me.*
**Student A:** *Why did you want to knit?*
**Student B:** *I wanted to learn how to make scarves for my friends.*

What do you usually do in your free time?
- When…?
- Where…?
- Why…?

What is your favorite thing to do outdoors?
- Where…?
- What…?
- Why…?

Do you like to travel?
- Where…?
- When…?
- Why…?

What is your favorite food?
- Where…?
- How…?
- Why…?

**PART 2** ● Now, make your own discussions! Choose one of the topics below, ask a question about that topic, then ask at least three follow up questions.

- Music
- Sports
- Movies and Television
- Friends and Family
- University or Job

# B. I Used To Wear a Tutu

## Language Point : Talking About Past Habits and Situations

What was your favorite childhood pastime?

**Used to** expresses a repeated action in the past.
▸ I **used to** play soccer every day when I was in high school.

**Didn't use to** expresses something that was not routine in the past but is now.
▸ He **didn't use to** like dancing as much as he does now.

### Pre-listening

Look at the picture.
- What is something Grandpa Charles used to do?
- What is something Grandma Martha used to do?
- What is something their son Richard used to do but denies?

### Listening  TRACK 2-3

### Post-listening

What kinds of activities do you think your parents used to do when they were your age?
- Do you do any of the same activities now?

What activities did you use to do but don't do anymore?
- Why did you stop?

# C. Then and Now

**PART 1** ● Discuss what Susan used to do and how it's changed from what she does now.

> **Example:**
> Susan used to be an assistant chef, but now she owns her own catering company.

## Then

| | |
|---|---|
| Job | Assistant Chef |
| Hobby | Making short animated films |
| Friendship | Best friend Maggie |
| Favorite Food | Pasta |
| Health and Fitness | Relaxed, goes to the gym |
| Appearance and Fashion | Dyed hair, trendy clothing |
| Relationship | Married to Richard |

## Now

| | |
|---|---|
| Job | Owns her own catering company |
| Hobby | Watching old movies |
| Friendship | Best friend Linda |
| Favorite Food | Steak |
| Health and Fitness | Stressed, gained a little weight |
| Appearance and Fashion | Neat hair, professional clothing |
| Relationship | Still married to Richard |

**PART 2** ●

Look at the categories above. Discuss what you used to do 5, 10, or 20 years ago.
Compare what you used to do with what you do now. Why have things changed or stayed the same?

> **Example:**
> Ten years ago, I used to eat unhealthy foods like candy all the time. Now I still like candy, but I also eat plenty of healthy foods, like vegetables.

# Discussion Questions

**1** What are the most popular hobbies in your country today?
- ▶ What were the most popular hobbies in your country 25 years ago?
- ▶ What do you think will be some popular hobbies 25 years from now?

**2** Do you think cooking is a hobby or a **chore**? Why?
- ▶ Would you ever consider taking a cooking class?

**3** Do you think watching television is a relaxing activity or a waste of time? Why?
- ▶ What television programs did you use to watch when you were young?

**4** Have you ever collected anything special, such as stamps or coins? What did you collect?
- ▶ What kinds of items do you think might be useful to collect?

**5** Do you enjoy studying?
- ▶ What kinds of classes do you like to take for fun?

**6** How much free time do you have every week?
- ▶ How much free time would you like to have?

**7** If you had more free time, what would you do with it?

**8** What would you consider giving up in order to have more free time?

**chore** *(n.):* a task that one must do on a regular basis

# LESSON 2

## >> WARM UP

**Objectives:**
/ Go + verb + ing and Go + to

A. **Brainstorm as many activities and hobbies as you can think of.**

B. **Which activities from above do you think are...**

> ...fun?
> ...dangerous?
> ...unhealthy?
> ...safe?
> ...healthy?
> ...boring?

# A. Hobby Horse

**PART 1**

Discuss the people in the following pictures. What activities do they enjoy in their free time?

> **Example:**
> **A:** *What do you think Kat is doing?*
> **B:** *It looks like she's cooking. What else do you think Kat likes to do in her free time?*
> **C:** *Well, besides cooking, maybe she likes to read cookbooks and go out to new restaurants with friends.*
> **B:** *Maybe she cooked the meal in the picture for her friends.*

**Bill**

**Georgie**

**Frank**

**Rodney**

**Samantha**

**Ginger**

**Pam**

**Penny**

**Percy**

**Tina**

**Hilda**

**Ned**

**PART 2**

1. Which of these activities have you never done?
2. Which of these activities do you like? Which of these activities do you dislike?
3. Are there any activities in these pictures that you've been doing lately?
4. Are there any activities here that you want to do in the future?

Unit 1 All the time in the world | 17

# B. Let's Go Bowling!

## Language Point : Go + verb + ing and Go + to

**Go + verb + ing** is used in certain expressions about activities.
- I **go skiing** twice a month.
- I **went swimming** a lot last summer.
- Have you ever **gone scuba diving**?

**Go + to + location** is used to talk about going somewhere.
- I usually **go to** Big Mountain Resort on the weekend.

**Tip** It is **incorrect** to say I go to an activity.
*Incorrect: I go to skiing twice a month.*

**PART 1** ● Use the pictures to help you answer the questions below.

**Use *go + ing* in your answer. Use *go + to* for answering the follow up question.**

### What do the Thompsons like doing?

1. They go to a place in winter and move around on frozen water.
   - Where do they go when they want to enjoy this activity?
2. Lisa likes trying on outfit and buying shoes.
   - Where does she go when she wants to do these things?
3. Charles and Martha listen and move to the music.
   - Where do they go when they want to show off their moves?
4. Richard stays in one place and moves quickly on a machine.
   - Where does he go when he wants to exercise?
5. Jack gets into a hole filled with water and moves from one side to the other.
   - Where does he go when he wants to do this?

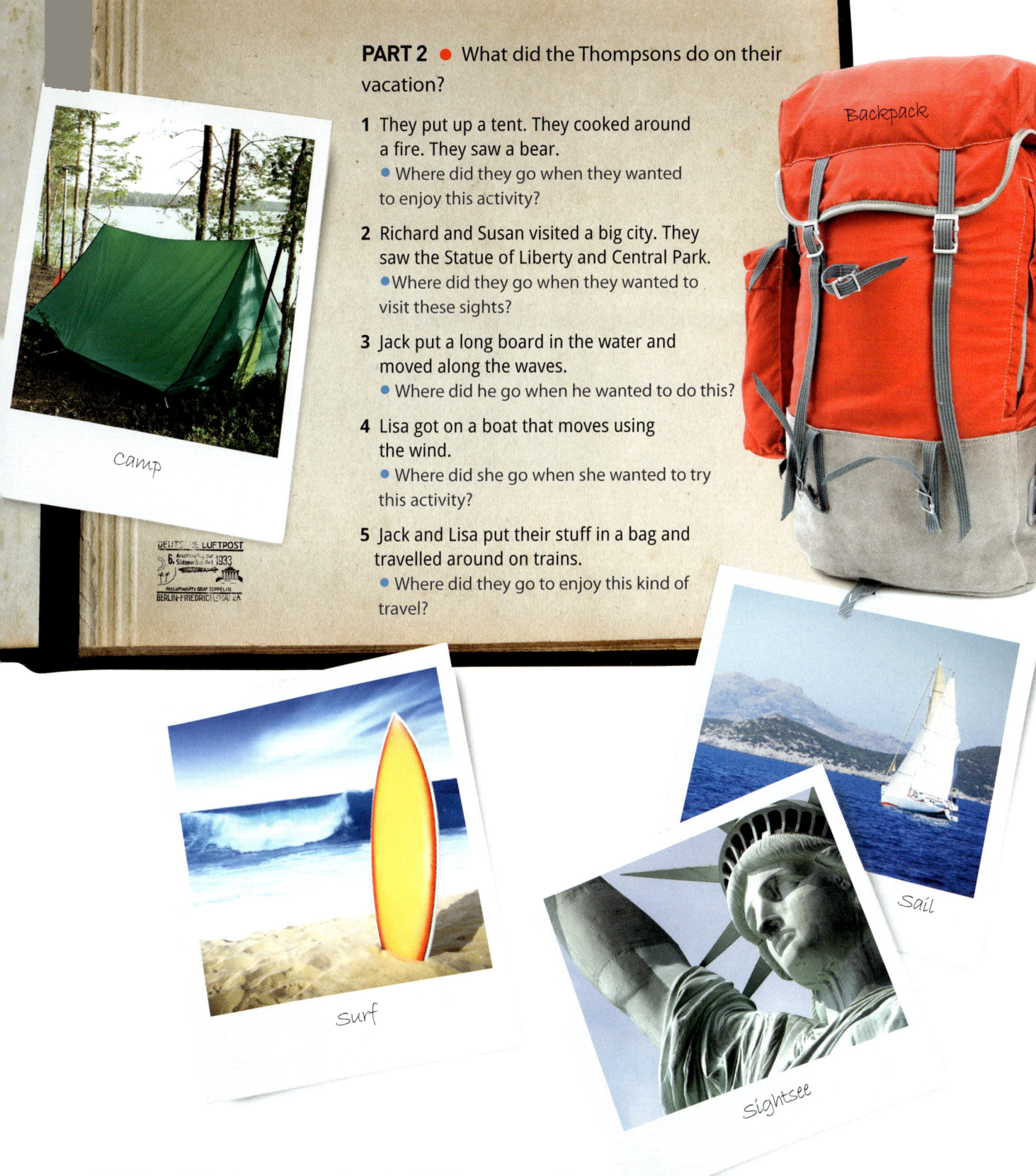

**PART 2** ● What did the Thompsons do on their vacation?

1 They put up a tent. They cooked around a fire. They saw a bear.
   ● Where did they go when they wanted to enjoy this activity?

2 Richard and Susan visited a big city. They saw the Statue of Liberty and Central Park.
   ● Where did they go when they wanted to visit these sights?

3 Jack put a long board in the water and moved along the waves.
   ● Where did he go when he wanted to do this?

4 Lisa got on a boat that moves using the wind.
   ● Where did she go when she wanted to try this activity?

5 Jack and Lisa put their stuff in a bag and travelled around on trains.
   ● Where did they go to enjoy this kind of travel?

Camp

Backpack

Surf

Sightsee

Sail

**PART 3** ● Talk about yourself, and ask follow up questions.

1 Which of the above activities have you done?
   ● Where did you go to do this activity?

2 Which ones have you never done?

3 Which ones would you like to try?
   ● Where would you want to go to try it?

Unit 1 All the time in the world | 19

# C. What Would You Do?

**PART 1** • If you had a free weekend, what would you do in the following locations?

**Example:**

**A:** *If I had a free weekend in an oceanside town, I would definitely start by going parasailing. After that, I might try going surfing because I love being active.*

**B:** *Wow…I prefer relaxing, so I would probably sit on the beach all day every day.*

arcade (n.): a place where people go to play video games

## PART 2

Imagine that you and your partner(s) are spending a weekend together at one of the locations on pages 20 and 21. Discuss what you would like to do, and create a schedule for your weekend.

**Example:**
**A:** *Where would you like to go?*
**B:** *Let's go to the park.*
**C:** *Okay. We could go swimming Saturday afternoon.*

|           | Saturday | Sunday |
|-----------|----------|--------|
| Morning   |          |        |
| Afternoon |          |        |
| Night     |          |        |

# Discussion Questions

1. What are the good and bad sides of extreme activities, such as bungee jumping and skydiving?

2. Do you enjoy outdoor activities, such as camping and hiking? Why or why not?
   - ▶ Would you say that you're an **outdoorsy** person?

3. Where do you hope to go during your next vacation?
   - ▶ Why would you like to go there?

4. Some people like **staycations**. Would you consider a staycation to be relaxing?
   - ▶ What can you do to occupy your time on a staycation?

5. Where is your favorite place to go in your city? Why?
   - ▶ How often do you get to go there?

6. Do you think that playing video games is a fun hobby or a bad habit?
   - ▶ What good things are there about playing video games?
   - ▶ What negative things are there about playing video games?

7. What are the good and bad sides of going drinking in your free time?
   - ▶ Do you like to go drinking with friends during your free time?
   - ▶ If you don't like to go drinking, what do you like to do instead of drinking?

## UNIT 1 REVIEW

**How well can you use:**
- ☐ Use to for talking about past habits and situations?
- ☐ Go + verb + ing and go + to?

What do you need to study more?

**outdoorsy** *(adj.)*: well suited to an outdoor environment
**staycation** *(idiom)*: a vacation that does not involve traveling

## Activity: Bingo! Have you ever…

Find people in your class who have had the experiences below. When you ask questions, be sure to modify verb forms so that they are correct.

# BINGO

### Have you ever…

| go bungee jumping  Name | water ski  Name | catch a fish  Name | get lost  Name | get a scholarship  Name |
|---|---|---|---|---|
| fire a gun  Name | break a bone  Name | have a nightmare  Name | go on a roller coaster  Name | go to the beach in the winter  Name |
| play golf  Name | wear glasses  Name | find money on the street  Name | see a movie star  Name | travel by plane  Name |
| miss an exam  Name | be in love  Name | climb a mountain  Name | propose marriage to someone  Name | speak to someone in another language outside of a classroom  Name |
| speak on the telephone in English  Name | ride a horse  Name | be in a car accident  Name | almost drown  Name | be in a cave  Name |

24 | SLE Generations 2B

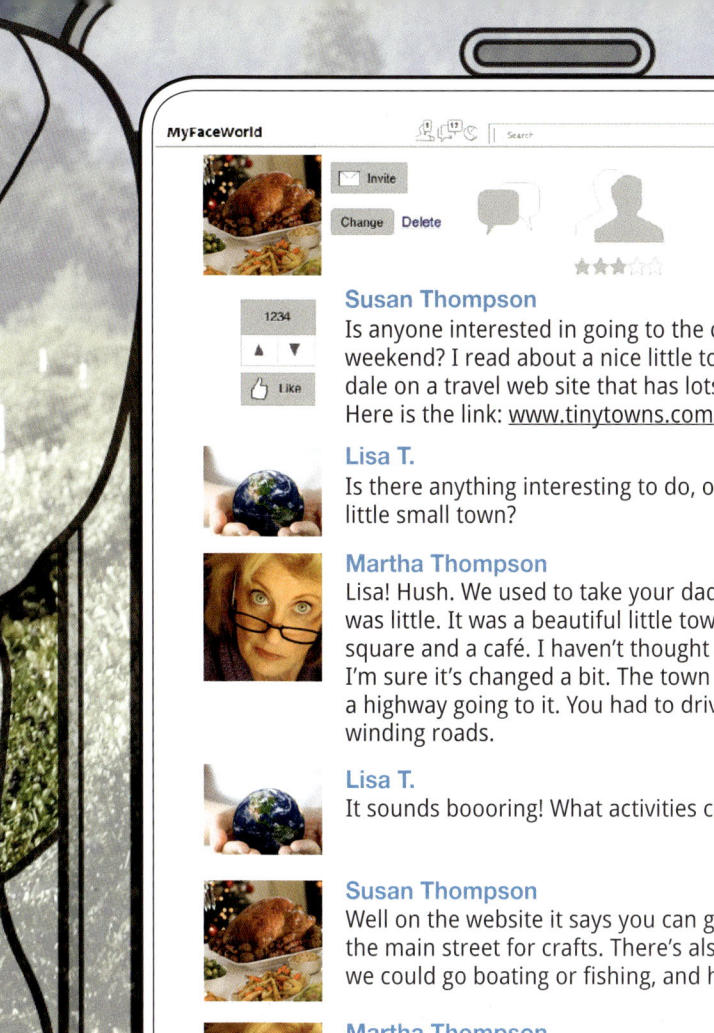

**Susan Thompson**
Is anyone interested in going to the countryside this weekend? I read about a nice little town called Idledale on a travel web site that has lots of things to do. Here is the link: www.tinytowns.com/getaways

**Lisa T.**
Is there anything interesting to do, or is it just a boring little small town?

**Martha Thompson**
Lisa! Hush. We used to take your dad there when he was little. It was a beautiful little town with an old town square and a café. I haven't thought about that in years! I'm sure it's changed a bit. The town didn't use to have a highway going to it. You had to drive over a lot of winding roads.

**Lisa T.**
It sounds boooring! What activities can we do?

**Susan Thompson**
Well on the website it says you can go shopping along the main street for crafts. There's also a small lake where we could go boating or fishing, and have a picnic.

**Martha Thompson**
When we used to go, there was a blueberry farm where you could pick blueberries for a small fee. Richard loved going berry picking. After we went home, I would bake a pie.

**Lisa T.**
I know! You used to call him little piggy after he ate one of those pies and denied it!

**Richard Thompson**
Now hold on, Lisa. That was never proven to be me!

**Martha Thompson**
Some things never change, Richard. Let's go to Idledale and see if that blueberry farm is still there.

### A. Discussion

1. Where do you typically go with your family on the weekend, or when you have free time?
   ▶ How is what you do now with your family different from what you used to do when you were younger?

2. What activities do you enjoy doing with your friends as opposed to your family?
   ▶ Are there things that you didn't use to do that you spend a lot of time doing now?

3. Richard's parents used to call him by a **nickname**. Did you or anyone you know use to have a nickname when you were younger? How did you get the name?

### B. Writing

Write a short story (a paragraph) about a short trip you went on as a child. Where did you go? What did you do there? How has the place you went to changed?

# 02
# The Numbers Game
*Vague and Precise*

**Objectives:**
/ Vague and precise descriptions
/ Listen to a story about a new job

# WARM UP

**In what situations are you general or specific about the following topics?**

*I would be vague when…*
*I would be precise when…*

| | |
|---|---|
| • Weight | • Work |
| • Age | • Birthday presents |
| • Education | • Food |

### PHRASAL VERBS

- **Look over**
  If you *look over* your work, it will be more precise.
- **Figure out**
  They can't *figure out* what's going on in the picture.

### IDIOMS

- **(word)-ish**
  Let's meet for coffee at *sixish*.
- **Beat around the bush**
  He needs to stop *beating around the bush* and be specific!
- **Give or take**
  The car will cost $10,000, *give or take* a few dollars.

### COLLOCATIONS

- **On time**
  I'm always *on time* for class because I'm an excellent student!

### TONGUE TWISTER

One-One was a racehorse.
Two-Two was one, too.
One-One won one race.
Two-Two won one, too.

# LESSON 1

## A. You Know What I Mean?

**Language Point:** Vague and Precise Language
We use vague language when we are not sure or do not need to be exact.
We use precise language when it is important to give an exact amount or description.

### VAGUE
**About** + number
**Around** + number or location
**Kind of** + adjective

### PRECISE
**Precisely** + number
**Right** + preposition
**Definitely** + adjective

---

### VAGUE

The party starts at *about* six.
I'll be there after that.

It's *around* the station.
Call me when you arrive.

The party is *kind of* dressy.
Wear something nice.

**Time**

**Location**

**Descriptions**

### PRECISE

The party starts *precisely* at six.
We shouldn't be late.

It's *right* next to the station.
Go out the exit and it's on the left.

The party is *definitely* formal.
A tux or evening dress is required.

Give vague answers to the questions on the left. Give precise answers to the questions on the right.

# VAGUE

# PRECISE

## 1

Where is the movie theater?
How long is the movie?
Was the main character good-looking?

## 2

Where did you sit in the theater?
How much did your ticket cost?
What exactly did the main character look like?

## 3

How long did you stay in Paris?
Where was your hotel?
How was the food?

## 4

How long were you in Paris?
Where was your hotel?
How long did you wait in line at the Eiffel Tower?

## 5

How late does the museum stay open?
What is there to see?
Where is the gift shop?

## 6

What time does the museum close?
How many tours are done on Saturdays?
Where do the tours start?

# B. Rock Starish

### Did You Know?
- We use vague language when we are not sure about or don't want to give information.
- We use precise language to stress confidence in our knowledge of the information.

### Pre-listening
How much money would you need to...

- Move out?
- Travel around the world?
- Buy a house?
- Buy all your friends dinner?

### Listening  TRACK 4-5
Listen to find out which topics Jack was vague and precise about. Check the box below as you listen.

|  | Vague | Precise |
|---|---|---|
| Job |  |  |
| Pay |  |  |
| Saving |  |  |

### Post-listening

1. What are some good part-time jobs for students?
   - Have you ever worked a part-time job to make money? What did you do?

2. How much money did Jack's parents say he needed to have before he could move out?
   - How much did his parents say he would need to raise before they would help him?

3. Do you think it's a good idea for children to move out of their parents' home after they graduate from university or should they wait until getting married?
   - When do you think someone should move out on their own?

# C. A Thousand and One Things

## Language Point: Expressing General Amounts

Fractions and percentages-
**Percentages and fractions are often used to express numerical information.**

Male Applicants
**48%** of the applicants are male

In speaking, both percentages and fractions are frequently **rounded** to the closest whole number.
49% of the applicants are male → Around fifty percent/About half of the applicants are male.

**PART 1** • Look at the pictures below and describe your observations using fractions and percentages.

### Example:
- *Two thirds of the women are wearing black dresses.*
- *60% of the people in this picture are women.*
- *About half of the people in this picture are wearing ties.*
- *100% of the people in this picture are holding glasses.*

**round** *(v.)*: to express a complex number by expressing the whole number above or below it

## PART 2

Survey your classmates! Use fractions and percentages to report the information you find. Ask follow up questions to learn more about your classmates.

| Question ✓ | Notes / Statistics Found |
|---|---|
| **1. Have you ever traveled abroad?**<br>☐ A. No, I have never traveled abroad.<br>☐ B. Yes, I have traveled abroad.<br><br>Follow up: How many continents have you visited? | A: 6 students<br>B: 5 students<br><br>About fifty percent of the students in this class have traveled abroad.<br><br>Around half of the students in this class have never traveled abroad. |
| **2. What is your favorite movie genre?**<br>☐ A. Action/adventure<br>☐ B. Comedy<br>☐ C. Romance<br>☐ D. Other _____<br><br>Follow up: How often do you go to the movies? | A:<br>B:<br>C:<br>D: |
| **3. Do you have a pet?**<br>☐ A. No, I do not have a pet.<br>☐ B. Yes, I have a cat.<br>☐ C. Yes, I have a dog.<br>☐ D. Yes, I have _____<br><br>Follow up: Do animals relieve stress? | A:<br>B:<br>C:<br>D: |
| **4. How do you usually take notes in class?**<br>☐ A. I don't take notes in class.<br>☐ B. I usually take notes with a pencil.<br>☐ C. I usually take notes with a pen.<br>☐ D. I usually type my notes.<br><br>Follow up: Ask your own. | A:<br>B:<br>C:<br>D: |
| **5. Ask your own question!**<br><br>Follow up: Ask your own. | |

# Discussion Questions

1 What is your favorite number? Why?

2 Approximately how much vacation time do you get each year?
   ▶ Exactly how much vacation time would you like every year?

3 If you had around $10,000 to spend and **roughly** three weeks off, where would you go and what would you do?

4 Do you think it's better to be vague or precise during a job interview? Why?

5 In what types of professions is it important to be precise?

6 **Give or take** a few minutes, how long does it take you to get to this class?

7 Would you consider yourself to be a **detail-oriented** person? Why or why not?

8 Do you have to write things down to remember them or can you remember specific details?

**detail-oriented** *(adj.)*: able to focus on the small aspects of a matter
**give or take** *(idiom)*: expresses approximate information
**roughly** *(adverb)*: denotes that a number is not exact, but rather is an estimation

# LESSON 2

>> WARM UP

**Objectives:**
/ Prepositions of time

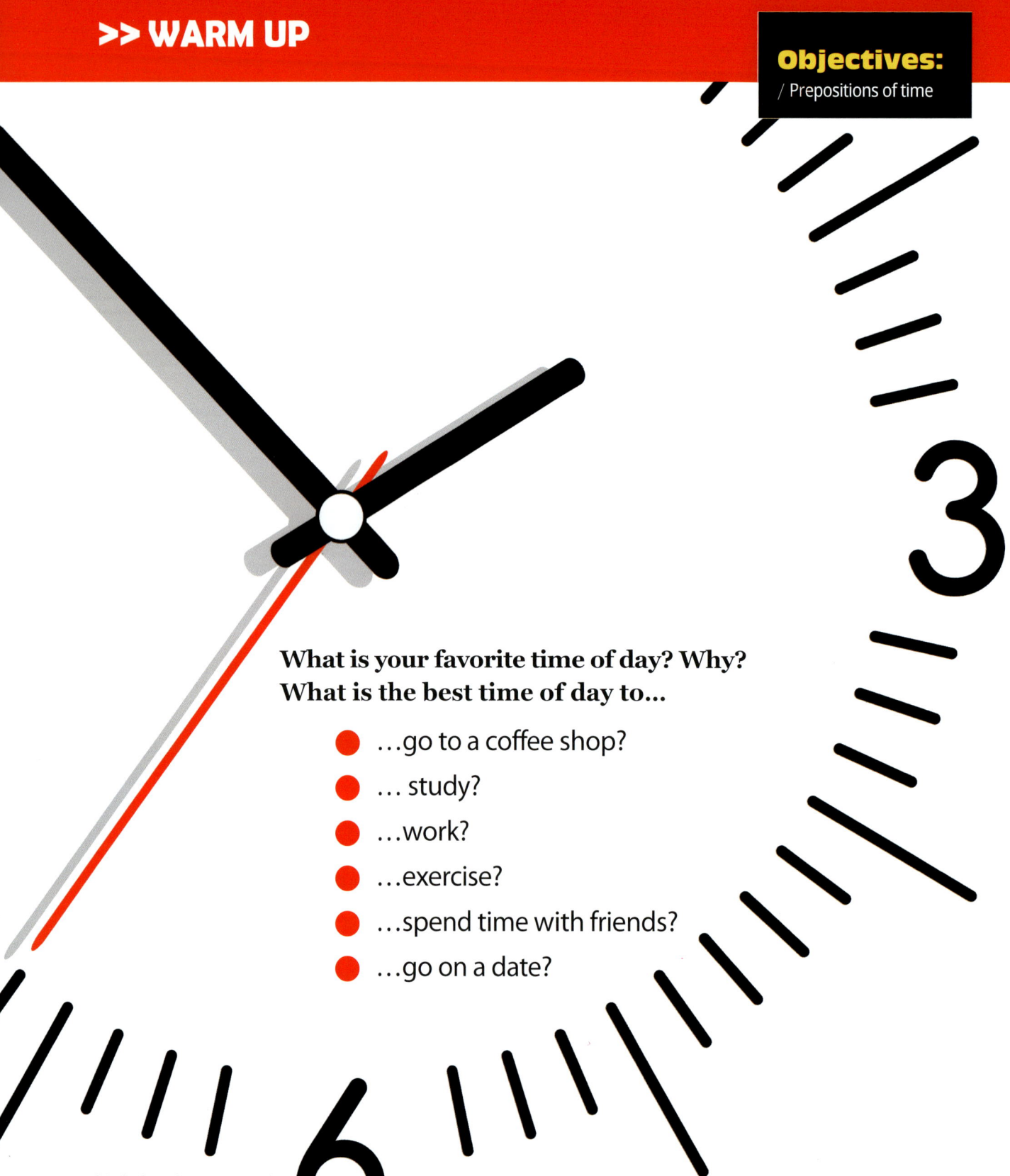

What is your favorite time of day? Why?
What is the best time of day to…

- …go to a coffee shop?
- … study?
- …work?
- …exercise?
- …spend time with friends?
- …go on a date?

# A. Always on Time

**Do You Remember?**
- *Around* and *About* are used when describing a non-specific amount.

## Language Point : Prepositions of Time

**Prepositions of time : a specific point**

**On** is used with days.
▶ I'll see you **on** Christmas. It's **on** a Saturday this year.

**In** is used with months, years, seasons, and times of day.
▶ It happened **in** the afternoon **in** July **in** 2005.

**At** is used with an exact time of day. (**at night** is an exception)
▶ I go to work **at** 7 p.m. I usually finish **at** midnight.

**Prepositions of time : extended period**

**From-to** is used with two points of time.
▶ The band will play **from** seven **to** nine.

**For** is used with a length of time.
▶ I'm in town **for** the next week and a half.

**Until** is used with an end time.
▶ I'll be here **until** the 14th.

### PART 1

Put the correct preposition in the space. Ask the questions, and ask a follow up question.

1. What do you like to do _____ the morning?
2. What things do people usually do _____ night?
3. What did you do _____ New Year's Eve last year?
4. _____ when _____ when do you go to school/work every day?
5. _____ how many days will you go on your next vacation?
6. What season were you born _____?

### PART 2   Answer the questions about Lisa's weekend in full sentences.

|  | Saturday | Sunday |
|---|---|---|
| **Morning** | 10 a.m. woke up/ 11 a.m. ate pancakes | Slept in |
| **Afternoon** | 1-5 p.m. went shopping with friends | Noon woke up<br>1p.m. ate lunch with family |
| **Night** | 8 p.m. ate dinner with Biff<br>10 p.m.-1 a.m. went clubbing | 6-9 p.m. watched TV<br>12 a.m. went to sleep |

1. What time of day did Lisa wake up on Saturday?
   - Did Lisa go shopping in the morning or in the afternoon? How long did she shop?
   - What things did Lisa spend her time doing after shopping?
   - What time did she stay at the club until?
2. What did Lisa do early the next day?
   - What time of day did she wake up, and what did she do after that?
   - What did she do starting at six and ending at nine?
   - When did she go to bed? Was it early or late?

**sleep in (phrasal verb):** to sleep longer than is typical

# B. Band Aid

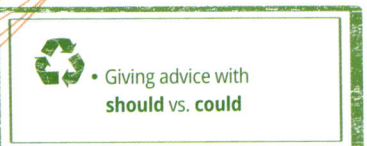
• Giving advice with **should** vs. **could**

Jack is trying to make extra money as the manager of the Crimson Kings. Help Jack by deciding when and where the band can fit everything into their busy schedules. Consider their availability and the business hours on the next page.

**Example:**
**A:** Well, they could shop for new guitars at Guitar World **on** Friday **at** 3.
**B:** But Paul is at work **from** 11 **to** 7.
**C:** Hmmm....in that case, they should go **on** Sunday **at** 11.

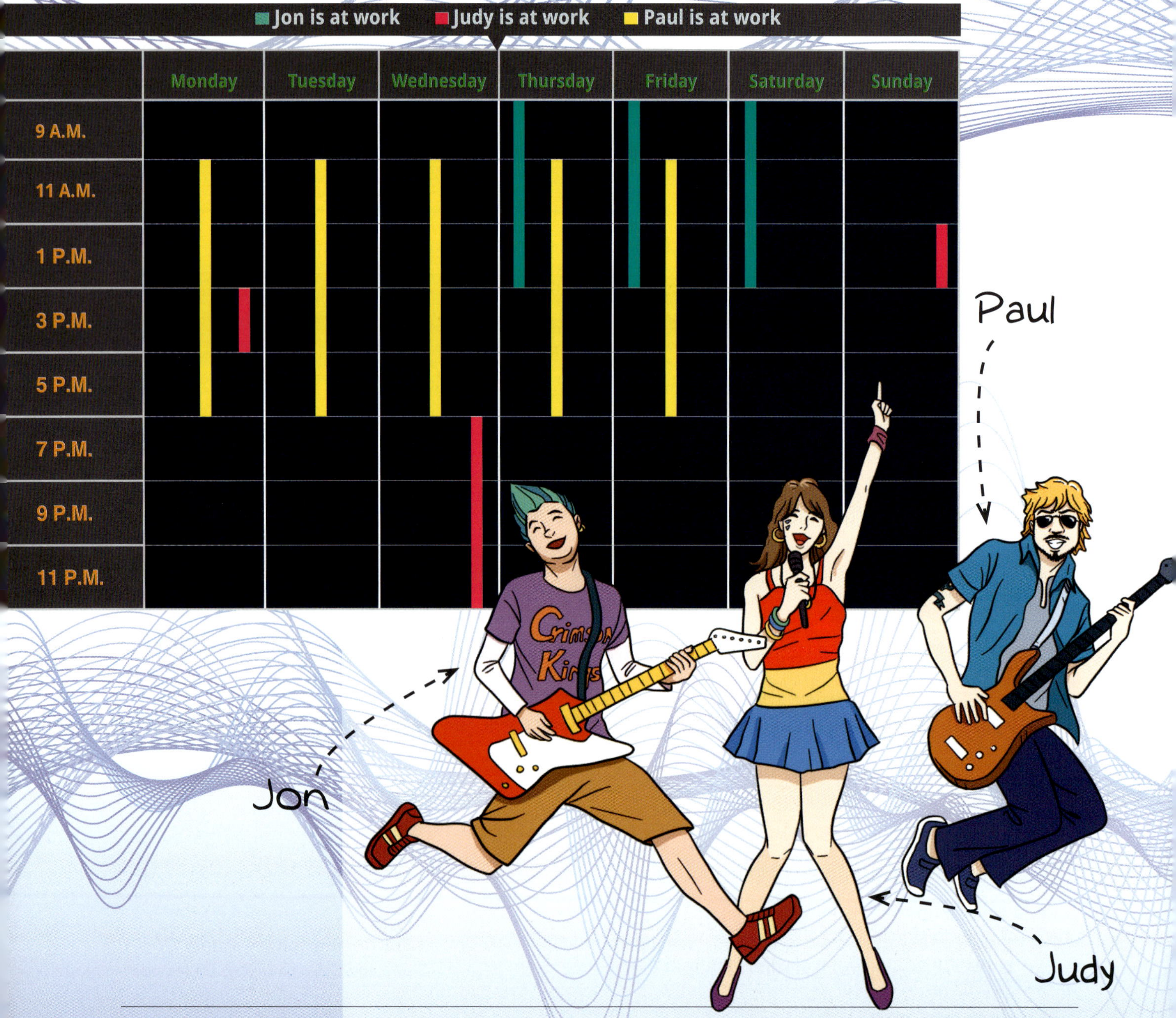

**autograph** *(n.)*: a famous person's signature
**duet** *(n.)*: a musical piece performed by two musicians
**gig** *(n.)*: a job a performer gets

# To-do List

**All of the band members need to do the following things together:**
- Shop for new guitars (1 hour)
- Shop for new clothes (2 hours)
- Practice three times a week (1 hour/practice)
- Play two **gigs** at the local bar (2 hours each)
- Record a song (2 hours)
- Meet with fans and sign **autographs** at the music store (3 hours)
- Have a photo shoot (1 hour)

**John and Paul need to practice a duet together (1 hour)**

- **Hum Depot (recording and practice space)**
  Monday - Friday 9 a.m. to 11 p.m., closed weekends

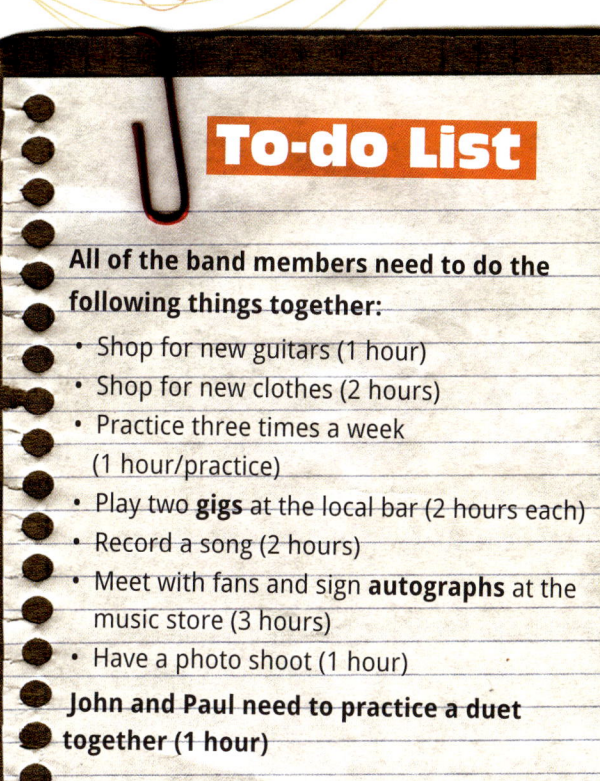

- **Guitar World - big sale**
  Friday 11 a.m. to 9 p.m., Saturday 11 a.m. to 7 p.m., Sunday 11 a.m. to 7 p.m.

- **Sound Warehouse (music store)**
  Monday - Sunday 9 a.m. to 9 p.m.

- **The Stinky Peanut**
  7 p.m. to 1 a.m., closed Monday

- **Shutterbug (photo studio)**
  9 a.m. to 9 p.m., Saturdays and Sundays only

- **Tight and Black (a rock boutique)**
  10 a.m. to 7 p.m., closed Sunday

# C. Event Planner

You work for a company that helps your **clients** plan for special occasions such as birthday parties, weddings, concerts, and team-building events.

- Choose a client from the list and use the resources to develop an event based on the **client, the number of people involved, and the amount of money they can spend**.
- Not every event needs the same kinds of planning. For example, the team building event probably doesn't need advertising.

**Example:**
Let's have a Friday night event at a small local bar. We'll put out flyers around the university with the cover of their new album, "Underwater Blues", and their MyFaceWorld link. We'll have a seafood buffet as a theme to go along with the album title and three dancers dressed up like squid.

| Client | The Crimson Kings | Budget: $600 |
|---|---|---|
| | Choice | Cost |
| Venue | Bitter End Bar | $100 |
| Advertising | Black and White Photocopies | $50 |
| Add-ons | Dancers (x3), Seafood Buffet | $400 |
| | | Total cost: *$550* |

**Your event:**

| Client | | |
|---|---|---|
| | Choice | Cost |
| Venue | | |
| Advertising | | |
| Add-ons | | |
| | | Total cost: |

**client** (n.): a person or group that receives service or products

## Possible Clients:

| Client | # of people | Budget | Additional Info |
|---|---|---|---|
| Timmy's Twelfth Birthday Bash | 12 children, 4 adults | $600 | |
| Sombra Corporation Team Building Weekend | 19 people | $1,000 | |
| The Marriage of Edward Dean to Susannah Holmes, Reception Party | 184 people | $1,500 | |
| The Retirement Party of Ted Earnshaw | 32 people | $600 | |
| The Rubber Bottle Band Fundraising Concert for Cute Animals | As many as possible | $2,000 | Musicians have already volunteered to perform |

☐ **The Bitter End Bar**
- capacity: 40
- cost: $100

☐ **Callahan's Family Restaurant**
- capacity: 200
- cost: $300

**Venue**

☐ **Rose Concert Hall**
- capacity: 500
- cost: $500

☐ **Criswell Park**
- capacity: 1,000
- cost: Free under 50 people, $200 if over 50 people.

---

**team-building** *(adj.)*: intended to build relationships between the members of a group

## Advertisement:

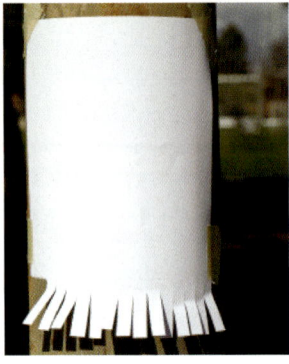

☐ Black and white photocopies
- cost: $50

☐ Advertisement in local paper
- cost: $100

☐ Radio spot
- cost: $400

☐ Internet campaign
- cost: $700

## Add-ons:

☐ Dancers
- cost: $50 per dancer

☐ Buffet
- cost: $10 per attendee

☐ Musicians (Jazz, classical, rock, etc.)
- cost: $100 per performer

☐ Light show and **pyrotechnics**
- cost: $300

**pyrotechnics** *(n.)*: fireworks display during a performance

# Discussion Questions

1 Are you more of a **morning person** or a **night owl**? Why?

2 Would you rather have flexible working hours, or have very specific working hours? Why?
   ▶ What would be your ideal working hours?

3 What is the best time of day to take the subway or ride the bus?
   ▶ When is **rush hour**?
   ▶ Do you enjoy taking public transportation during rush hour?

4 For you, what is the best time of day to do work or study? When are you most productive? Least productive?

5 Are you usually on time for appointments, or do you run late?

6 Which season is your favorite? Why?
   ▶ Which season were you born in?
   ▶ What sorts of activities do you like to do during your favorite season?

7 Some people enjoy planning parties and events such as weddings, while others consider event planning to be a chore.
   ▶ What are the pros and cons of planning your own events?
   ▶ If you have an event, would you rather plan it yourself or hire an event planner?

## UNIT 2 REVIEW

**How well can you use:**
- ☐ Vague and precise expressions to describe situations?
- ☐ Prepositions of time?

What do you need to study more?

**morning person** *(n.)*: a person who enjoys the morning
**night owl** *(n.)*: a person who enjoys nighttime and thrives at this time
**rush hour** *(n.)*: the period of time when people travel to and from work

# Activity: Night on the Town!

Your class has decided to plan a movie night together! Work together to decide on all the details of the night. For a decision to be accepted, a 60% majority is required.

| | |
|---|---|
| **1 Location of the movie night**<br>A. Movie theater<br>B. Classroom<br>C. Classmate's house | A:<br>B:<br>C: |
| **2 Budget**<br>A. $2/person<br>B. $10/person<br>C. $20/person | A:<br>B:<br>C: |
| **3 Theme**<br>A. Dinosaurs<br>B. Celebrities<br>C. Neon colors<br>D. Ugly sweater | A:<br>B:<br>C:<br>D: |
| **4 Movies to watch**<br>A. Comedy<br>B. Horror<br>C. Drama<br>D. Children's | A:<br>B:<br>C:<br>D: |
| **5 Snacks/food**<br>A. Eat out at a restaurant<br>B. Order pizza<br>C. Chips/popcorn<br>D. **BYOB** | A:<br>B:<br>C:<br>D: |

BYOB (adj.): being a party or event which guests are expected to bring their own beverages

Gig Space.com

# band bios
## Segue

### The Crimson Kings

"We want to play music and meet cool people, make some money, and not live with our parents. Anything you can do to help with these four things would be greatly appreciated, especially the third one."

**Judy**
**lead vocals, guitar**

**Statement** Has been playing guitar for about three weeks. Was accepted to Big U. in the spring, but decided to start a band instead. Is convinced that one third of the band does 75 percent of the work. Won a bunch of gold medals for outstanding hair style. Loses her cell phone exactly 42 times every day. Is trying to get the guys to let her cat write their next single.

**Paul**
**drums**

**Statement** Has precisely three tattoos that make him look cooler than everyone else in the band (not that it's hard to do). Still has health insurance (aka a day job). But turns into a drum playing animal at night. Has been wearing a mustache since he was old enough to walk. Voted "Most Likely to Play Drums" by 66 percent of the other members in his band.

**Jon**
**bass guitar**

**Statement** Sleeps around 12 hours a night because he hates being awake in the morning. Came second in the "Most Likely to Play Drums" contest with only 33 percent of the vote because he doesn't play drums. Likes to jam from dusk to dawn and aspires to one day live right next door to your house so he can rock you all night long!

Check us out at the Stinky Peanut bar and grill this Saturday night at 10 p.m. and on our new album "Blue Cat Blues", which will be out on the 25th of the month.

### A. Discussion

1. Who is your favorite singer/band?
   ▶ What interesting facts do you know about them?
   ▶ How long have they been making music?
   ▶ Have you ever seen them live? When was it, exactly?
2. Why is it important for a band, artist, or actor to promote themselves?
   ▶ What's the best way to do this in your opinion?

### B. Join the Band!

The Crimson Kings have asked you to join the band. Write your own bio like the one above. Consider:
▶ What makes you different from everyone else?
▶ What can you bring to the band?
▶ What is something interesting about you?

# 03
# Communication Breakdown
## Rumors and Misunderstandings

**Objectives:**
/ Checking and confirming information
/ Listen to a story about a misunderstanding

## WARM UP

Which resources would you use to learn about the topics below? You can choose more than one resource.

1. A popular new restaurant
2. The best university to study at abroad
3. A local store's customer service reputation
4. English classes at an institute
5. Hotels to stay at during your vacation
6. The best place to rent an apartment
7. Feeling sick to your stomach
8. Whether or not to break up with your boyfriend or girlfriend

**Possible Resources**
Internet
Friends
Parents
Travel agent
Coworker
Magazine
Professor
Doctor

### IDIOMS

- **Under the wrong impression**
  I think you're *under the wrong impression*. I never said I liked dogs.
- **Word of mouth**
  I didn't read that news anywhere. I heard it by *word of mouth*.

### PHRASAL VERBS

- **Spot on**
  There are a lot of ugly rumors going around, and some of them are *spot on*.
- **Clear up**
  I think we're having a misunderstanding. Let me try to *clear it up*.

### COLLOCATIONS

- **Spread rumors**
- **No idea**
  I have *no idea* why you think that. Someone must have been *spreading rumors* about me.

# LESSON 1

## A. Checking and Confirming Information

**Language Point : Checking and Confirming Information**

The verb **"hear"** is used in the past to say you have knowledge of something like a rumor.....
*I heard (that) you went to Spain last year.*

The main verb is in the past even if the verb in the clause is in the future.
*I heard (that) you are going to Spain next year.*

The verb **"tell"** is used to express information that someone shared. It is followed by an object.
*Someone told me (that) you are going to Spain next year.*

> **Tip**
> The reporting verb is often used informally in the present.
> *I **hear** (that) you are going to Spain on vacation.*

**confirm** *(v.)*: to verify

46 | SLE Generations 2B

Tell your partner what you heard or were told about the people in the pictures. Then, ask a follow up question.

**Example:**

**A:** *I heard that Cindy Lou ran away to become famous in Hollywood!*

**B:** *Really? How do you know she's going to California?*

**A:** *My sister's boyfriend's friend saw her on the highway with a sign that read: L.A.*

**Carrie**
I heard....

**Tim and Laddie**
Mr. J. told me.....

**Jenny and Craig**
I heard....

**Dorothy**
Aunt Mae told me..

**Sonni and Shar**
Mrs. Kim told me....

**Melvin**
I heard.....

**Murphey**
Murphey's boss told me...

**Thelma and Louise**
I heard....

# B. Say What?

**Pre-listening**

Who is your favorite band or singer?
What can you tell me about their background story?
Have you heard anything about them recently?

**Listening**  TRACK 6-7

While listening, cross out the misunderstood word and underline the correct word.

## Post-listening

1. Why did Jack have a problem understanding Grandma Martha?
   - What did Jack hear? What did Grandma actually say?
   - What did Grandma hear? What did Jack actually say?

2. Have you ever had a misunderstanding with someone when trying to speak another language?
   - What was the misunderstanding about?
   - How did you resolve it?

## PART 2 • Whispers

### Language Point: Correcting and Confirming Information

| Correcting | Confirming |
|---|---|
| I don't know where you heard that, but… | That's right. |
| Actually… | That's correct! |

- Whisper the information below to the person next to you.
- Pass the message along by whispers until the last person in the class has heard it.
- The last person is responsible for sharing the message that he or she heard with the class.
- Was anything misunderstood?

1. Your favorite television commercial
2. Something you were told to do when you were young
3. The best band of all time and what is your favorite song of theirs
4. Your favorite holiday
5. A description of your best friend
6. A dream you've had
7. The plot of your favorite movie
8. What you look for in the opposite sex

---

**correct** *(v.)*: to find and resolve an error/mistake

Unit 3 Communication Breakdown | 49

# C. A Little Bird Told Me...

- Choose one item from each of the following lists to create a character.
- Make a guess about your partner's character.
- Correct or confirm your partner's guess and add additional information to reveal your character's personality.
- Be sure to ask follow up questions.

**Example:**

**A:** *So I heard you are interested in politics!*

**B:** *Really? Who told you that? I'm actually interested in music.*

**A:** *Oh, I see. What kind of music do you like?*

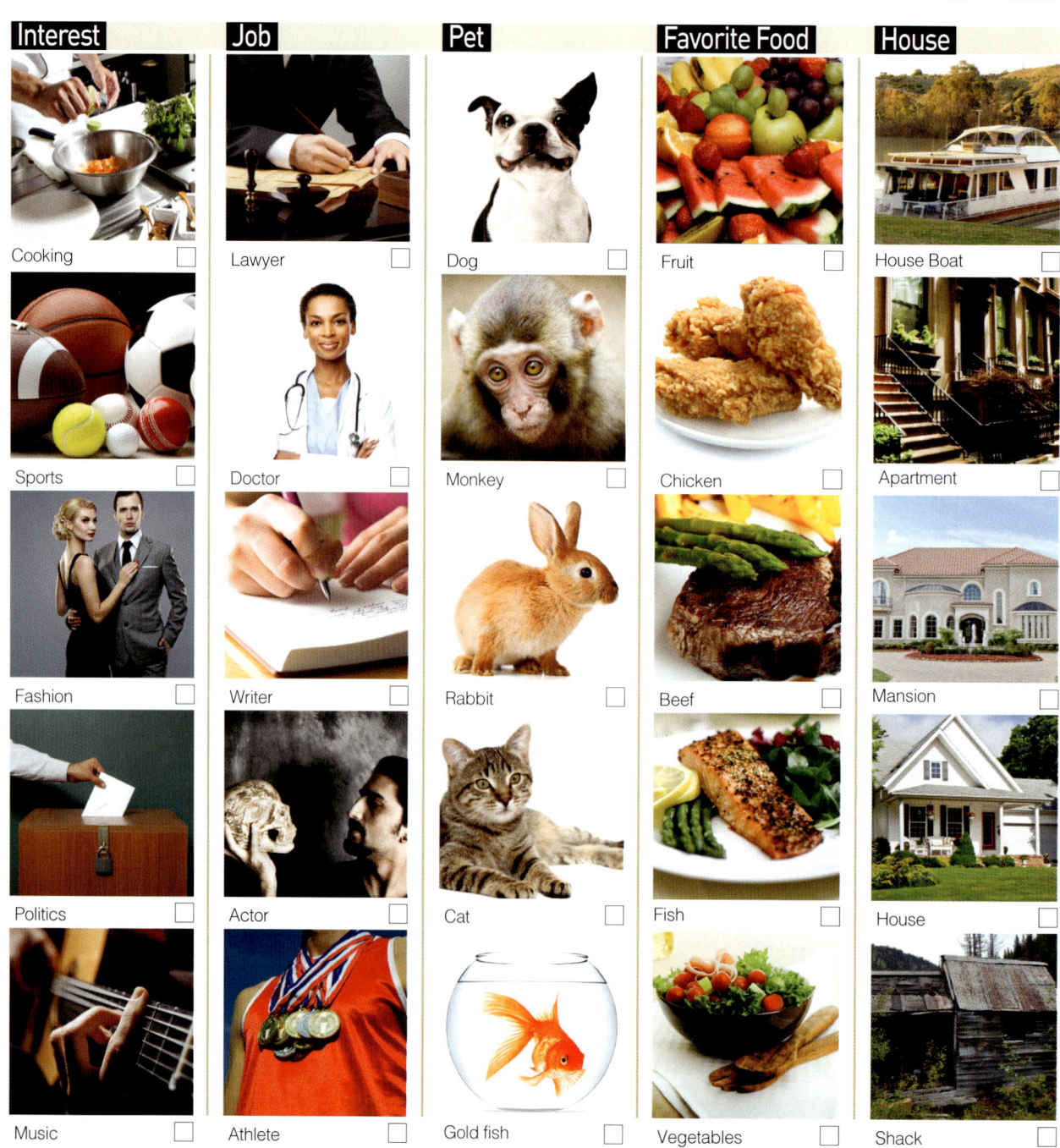

| Interest | Job | Pet | Favorite Food | House |
|---|---|---|---|---|
| Cooking ☐ | Lawyer ☐ | Dog ☐ | Fruit ☐ | House Boat ☐ |
| Sports ☐ | Doctor ☐ | Monkey ☐ | Chicken ☐ | Apartment ☐ |
| Fashion ☐ | Writer ☐ | Rabbit ☐ | Beef ☐ | Mansion ☐ |
| Politics ☐ | Actor ☐ | Cat ☐ | Fish ☐ | House ☐ |
| Music ☐ | Athlete ☐ | Gold fish ☐ | Vegetables ☐ | Shack ☐ |

# Discussion Questions

**1** Who do you think likes to gossip more: men or women?
- ▶ Why do you think so?

**2** Have you ever heard a **rumor** that you later discovered was untrue?
- ▶ What was the **rumor**?

**3** Have you ever heard a **rumor** that was **spot on**?
- ▶ What was the **rumor**?

**4** What kinds of things did your parents tell you when you were a child?
- ▶ If you are a parent, what is something that you try to tell your children often?
- ▶ If you do not have children, what is something that you would tell your child to do?

**5** Have you ever visited a **fortune teller?** If so, did you believe the things he or she told you?
- ▶ Do you think that some people believe everything they hear from fortune tellers? Why or why not?

**6** How has technology affected the way we hear news?
- ▶ What are some positive and negative effects of information technology?

**7** How many times do you usually have to be told something before you remember to do it?

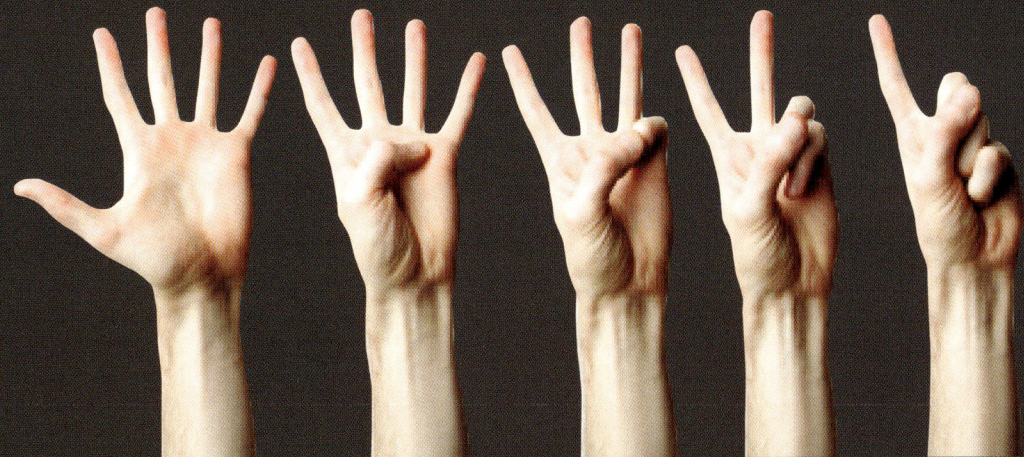

**fortune teller** *(n.)*: a person who attempts to predict others' futures
**rumor** *(n.)*: a piece of information that is spread around not supported by facts/data
**spot on** *(phrasal verb)*: exactly correct

# LESSON 2

## >> WARM UP

**Objectives:**
/ Resolving misunderstandings

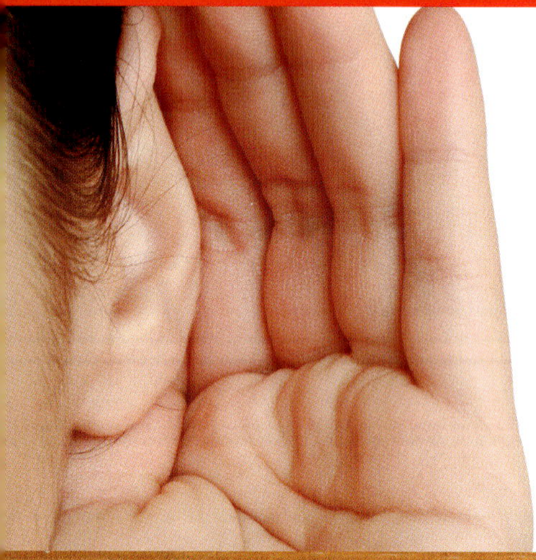

What did your teacher tell you in Unit 1?

What did you hear in Unit 2?

Unit 1 Lesson 1

Unit 1 Lesson 2

Unit 2 Lesson 1

Unit 2 Lesson 2

# A. That's Not What I Meant

## PART 1

Match each sentence to the correct picture, and discuss how the words in italics are different.

1 The *aisle* is empty.
2 The *isle* is empty.

3 No reading *aloud*.
4 No reading *allowed*.

5 It's a really dry *desert*.
6 It's a really dry *dessert*.

7 How much was the *fair*?
8 How much was the *fare*?

9 Dracula hates *stakes*.
10 Dracula hates *steaks*.

A

B

C

D

E

F

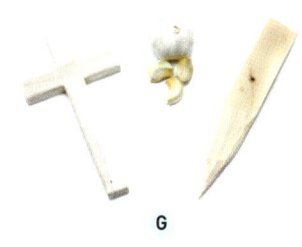
G

H

I

J

## Language Point : Resolving Misunderstandings

When misunderstandings happen, clarifying your meaning will help you to continue the conversation smoothly.

I think there's a misunderstanding.   What I actually said was...
What I meant was...   By _____, I mean _____.

## PART 2

- Take turns reading the statements on the left and choose only one of the **bold words** to say.
**Example:** She thinks she's going **today/to die.**
**A:** *She thinks she's going today.*

- Respond to your partner's statement with the question next to the **word** you heard.
**B:** *How long does she have to live?*

- **If** the question creates confusion, resolve the misunderstanding.
**A:** *I think there is a misunderstanding. What I meant was she's leaving now, today.*

1. We **can't/can** go to the movie tonight.
   → Can't  Why, is it sold out?
   → Can  Good. Can we meet there at six?

2. Jennie **hopped/hoped** to win the contest.
   → Hopped  Was it a jumping contest?
   → Hoped  Did she win or lose?

3. I'm allergic to **bees/peas**.
   → Bees  Have you ever been stung?
   → Peas  What about other vegetables?

4. The teacher is **collecting/correcting** the papers.
   → Collecting  Should I write my name at the top?
   → Correcting  Do you think you did well?

5. There is a big **duck/dock** in the lake.
   → Duck  What color are its feathers?
   → Dock  Are there any boats tied to it?

6. There are so many **fries/flies** on the plate.
   → Fries  Would you like some?
   → Flies  Do you want a new plate?

7. Don't **slip/sleep** on the floor.
   → Slip  Did someone spill something?
   → Sleep  Do you think it's too hard?

8. The **price/prize** was $1000.
   → Price  Does that include tax?
   → Prize  What was second place?

9. She went downstairs to get a **coffee/copy**.
   → Coffee  Isn't the café closed?
   → Copy  Why? Is the copier broken?

10. It's a little **noise/noisy**.
    → Noise  Can you not hear it?
    → Noisy  Should I turn it down?

# B. It's All Been One Big Misunderstanding

Work with a partner to act out the situations below. If your number says (START), begin the conversation. **Clear up** the misunderstanding.

> **Example:**
> **Student A:** *Do you like my company?*
> **Student B:** *Yes I do! I think it's great that you provide food for children in developing nations.*
> **Student A:** *I think there's a misunderstanding. By company, I mean…*

### 3rd wheel

If you are the third student in this activity, clear up the misunderstanding that the other two speakers are having.

(START) Ask your partner, **"Do you like my company?"**
(company = spending time with someone)

Give your partner advice on how to get rid of unwanted bugs.
(bug = insect)

(START) You are traveling around the UK. Ask your partner, **"How do you get to Wales in a car?"**
(Wales = a country in the United Kingdom)

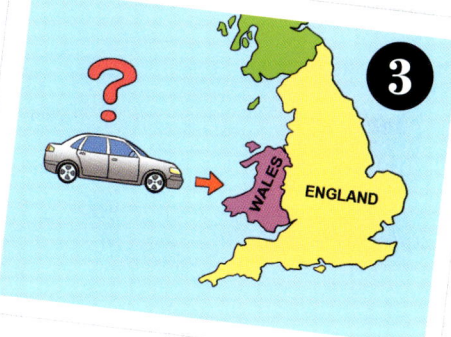

## STUDENT A

You love animals. Tell your friend that you're shocked that he or she bought a fur.
(fur = animal skin or hair)

(START) You had an appointment to eat at eight. You have been waiting for more than an hour. Tell your friend, **"I thought you were going to meet me here at eight!"**
(eight = 8 o'clock in the evening)

**clear up** *(phrasal verb)*: to resolve a misunderstanding

Work with a partner to act out the situations below. If your number says (START), begin the conversation. Clear up the misunderstanding.

> **Example:**
> **Student A:** *Do you like my company?*
> **Student B:** *Yes I do! I think it's great that you provide food for children in developing nations.*
> **Student A:** *I think there's a misunderstanding. By company, I mean…*

**STUDENT B**

1. Your partner works for a company that helps feed hungry children. Tell your partner what your opinion is of the company. (company = business or organization)

2. (START) You have a bug. Say to your friend, **"I have a bug. How can I get rid of it?"** (bug = illness)

3. You live in the UK. Your partner comes up to you on the street and asks you a strange question about whales. Tell your partner it's impossible. (whale = a large sea animal)

4. (START) Tell your partner, **"I bought a fir for Christmas."** (fir = a type of tree)

5. Tell your friend that you already ate. (ate = past tense of the verb "eat")

# C. International Job Swap

• Heard and told
• Tag questions

**Background:** You have decided to go on a "**working holiday**"! You have been invited to a party with people from many different countries who also want a "**working holiday**". Meet the people at the party and find someone to switch jobs with for a month.

Choose one of the party goers from the list. This will be **you**.
**Example: A:** (*Caleb*)
**B:** (*Betty*)

**Example:**

▶ **Introduce yourself to your partner.**
**A:** *Hi, nice to meet you. My name is Caleb.*
**B:** *Hi Caleb, my name is Betty.*

▶ **You only know a few rumors about the other person. Ask them if what you have heard is true.**
**B:** *So Caleb, You're a musician, aren't you?*

▶ **You will need to confirm or clarify the information your partner has heard.**
**A:** *I don't know where you heard that. Actually, I'm a **mortician**.*
**B:** *Oh, interesting! Have you always liked dead people?*

Then tell your partner something you have heard about them. If there is a _____, invent your own information.

## Party Goers A

**Betty**
**Job** Ski Instructor
**Rumor 1** Hates ____ (food)
**Rumor 2** Studies cats
**Country She Wants to Visit** Switzerland

**Elizabeth**
**Job** Clown
**Rumor 1** Despises ____ (color)
**Rumor 2** Has a garden
**Country She Wants to Visit** Spain

**Abraham**
**Job** Doctor
**Rumor 1** Loves hunting
**Rumor 2** Speaks ____ languages
**Country He Wants to Visit** Germany

**Caleb**
**Job** Mortician
**Rumor 1** Likes Meditation
**Rumor 2** Makes balloon animals
**Country He Wants to Visit** Australia

**Foy**
**Job** Window Washer
**Rumor 1** Likes eating cereal without milk
**Rumor 2** Born without a nose
**Country He Wants to Visit** USA

**mortician** *(n.):* someone who prepares a person's body after they have died
**working holiday** *(n.):* going on holiday and working at the same time

**Background:** You have decided to go on a "working holiday"! You have been invited to a party with people from many different countries who also want a "working holiday". Meet the people at the party and find someone to switch jobs with for a month!

Take on the role of one of the party goers below.
**Example:** A: (Caleb)
B: (Betty)

### Example:

**Introduce yourself to your partner.**
**A:** *Hi, nice to meet you. My name is Caleb.*
**B:** *Hi Caleb, my name is Betty.*

▶ **You only know a few rumors about the other person. Ask them if what you have heard is true.**
**B:** *So Caleb, you're a musician, aren't you?*

▶ **You will need to confirm or clarify the information your partner has heard.**
**A:** *I don't know where you heard that. Actually, I'm a mortician.*
**B:** *Oh, interesting! Have you always liked dead people?*

Then, tell your partner something you have heard about them. If there is a , invent your own information.

## Party Goers B

**Betty**
**Job** Ski instructor
**Rumor 1** Hates meat
**Rumor 2** Afraid of cats
**Country She Wants to Visit** Switzerland

**Elizabeth**
**Job** Actor
**Rumor 1** Doesn't like yellow
**Rumor 2** Has a garden
**Country She Wants to Visit** ____ (European country)

**Abraham**
**Job** Professor
**Rumor 1** Loves ____ (hobby)
**Rumor 2** Speaks twelve languages
**Country He Wants to Visit** Germany

**Caleb**
**Job** Musician
**Rumor 1** Likes Meditation
**Rumor 2** Makes ___ (object)
**Country He Wants to Visit** Australia

**Foy**
**Job** Cleaner
**Rumor 1** Likes eating cereal without milk
**Rumor 2** Born with a small nose
**Country He Wants to Visit** USA

# Discussion Questions

1 Which words do you find most difficult to pronounce in English?

2 If someone speaks to you in a foreign language and you have no idea what they said, what do you say to them?

3 In what kinds of situations do you think that information might get lost in translation?
   - ▶ Have you ever been in a situation where you felt like something was lost in translation? What happened?

4 How often do you have misunderstandings with friends, and how do you resolve them?

5 Have you ever been **under the wrong impression** when texting or instant messaging?
   - ▶ What was the misunderstanding about?

6 What are some common misunderstandings that people have when they visit your country?

7 In which jobs is it important to avoid misunderstandings?

## UNIT 3 REVIEW

**How well can you use:**
- ☐ Language for checking and confirming information?
- ☐ Language for resolving misunderstandings?

What do you need to study more?

**under the wrong impression** *(idiom):* describes someone who is misinformed

# Activity : Idioms

Match the idiom on the left to its literal meaning on the right. Then, discuss what you think the actual meaning of the idiom is and a situation in which you would use it.

## Idiom

1. Break a leg
2. Pulling my leg
3. Frog in your throat
4. Crying over spilled milk
5. Thinking outside the box
6. My foot fell asleep
7. Butterflies in your stomach
8. Get out of my face

## Literal

## Message Boards

# Segue

**Topic:** There was a misunderstanding.

**Martha227**

Hello ladies!
I'm posting about my grandson, Jack. He is involved with this band called the "Crimson Kings", and I think he's been doing some strange things. The other night he got home late, and when I asked him where he had been, he told me he slept on a wet floor! Why would he be sleeping on a wet floor when he's supposed to be working?
I told Susan that Jack needs to quit that job because it sounds like he's getting in trouble.

**Judith835**

Martha…do you think there was a misunderstanding? I know Jack can be a bit silly, but sleeping on a wet floor is strange, even for him. Do you think that's what he actually told you?

**Gladys 775**

Don't make Jack quit his job yet! I was thinking about what Jack said, and I agree with Judith. I think there was a misunderstanding. I think that what Jack actually told you was that he SLIPPED on the wet floor.

**Martha227**

Oh Gladys, that makes a lot of sense! I think you're right. I have been having a bit of trouble with my ears lately. How embarrassing! Now I'll have to check on him…I hope he isn't hurt, and I hope Susan didn't make him quit the job.

## A. Discussion
1. What incorrect information did Martha hear?
   Why did she misunderstand the information?
2. Have you ever heard a rumor that was incorrect?
3. If you heard a friend spreading a rumor that wasn't true, how would you clear up the misunderstanding?
   What would you say or do to avoid insulting the person who was spreading the rumor?

## B. Writing
Write a short paragraph on a rumor you have heard about someone you know or a famous celebrity.
Write about why you think the rumor may or may not be true.

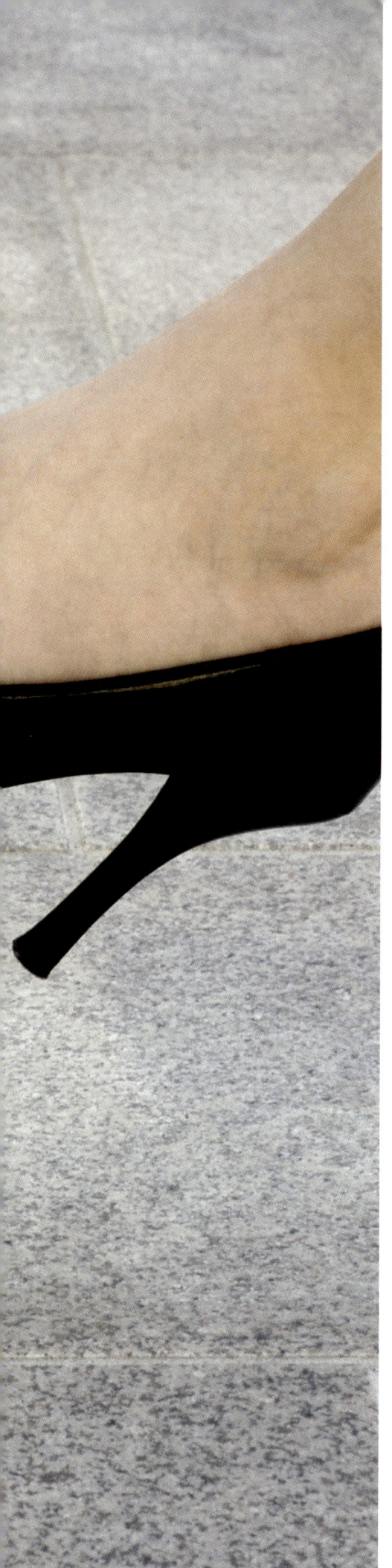

## WARM UP

**Brainstorm as many different natural disasters as you can think of.**

### COLLOCATIONS

- **Take precautions**
  Please make sure to *take precautions*, like fastening your seatbelt, before you drive a car.

### PHRASAL VERBS

- **To reach out**
  The disaster was terrible, but it gave us an opportunity to *reach out* and help one another.
- **Watch out**
  Be careful to *watch out* for pickpockets when visiting the city.

### IDIOMS

- **Better to be safe than sorry**
- **An accident waiting to happen**
  Putting the cup on the edge of the window is just an *accident waiting to happen*. Put it on the floor. It's *better to be safe than sorry*.
- **Keep your cool**
  Don't panic! *Keep your cool,* and walk slowly away from the bear.

### TONGUE TWISTER

The thirty-three thieves thought they thrilled the throne through Thursday.

There those thousand thinkers were thinking, where did those other three thieves go through.

Unit 4 Better Safe Than Sorry | 63

# LESSON 1

## A. What Do I Do?!

Discuss what solutions are possible for the personal emergencies below. Ask why you think it is a good solution.

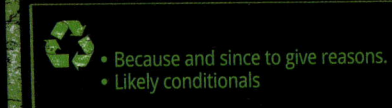
- Because and since to give reasons.
- Likely conditionals

**Example:** Animal Attack - You are walking in the park when a dog attacks you.

**A:** *What would you do?*
**B:** *If a dog attacked me, I'd grab it and take it with me to the hospital.*
**A:** *Really? Why?*
**B:** *To make sure it doesn't have rabies.*

### ACCIDENTS

1. **Car Crash** You are driving in the countryside when you come across a car that has hit a tree.
2. **Passport** You are traveling in a foreign country when you realize you have lost your passport.
3. **Phone** You get a new smart phone, but just a few hours later you drop it in a public toilet!

### SOCIAL EMERGENCIES

1. **Food Poisoning** You are out with your boyfriend or girlfriend having dinner when suddenly you become very ill.
2. **Wardrobe Malfunction** You bend down to pick up a pencil at work and your pants rip up the middle.
3. **Mr. Squiggles!** Your cat has climbed up a very tall tree and is too scared to climb back down.

## DISASTERS

1 **Gas Leak** You wake up in the night and smell a strong odor like rotten eggs coming from the kitchen.
2 **Grease Fire** Your friend is cooking something on the stove when suddenly the grease in the pan catches fire.
3 **Localized Flood** While driving to work, you try to cross an intersection that is full of water, and suddenly the car starts floating!

## CRIME

1 **Burglary** You come home from a weekend trip. You notice that the front door of your house is open.
2 **Hit and Run** You see a child crossing the street when she's hit by a scooter. The scooter driver **takes off**.
3 **Identity Theft** You get a call from your bank asking why you bought ten new computers yesterday.

**take off** *(phrasal verb)*: to run away suddenly and quickly

Unit 4 Better Safe Than Sorry | 65

# B. When It Rains, It Pours

It rained forty days and forty nights at the Thompson household. What was damp became a puddle. A puddle became a pool. A pool became a small lake.

## Pre-listening

Imagine that you just found out that your entire house is going to flood within an hour. You can only take three things with you.
What would you choose?

_____
_____
_____

## Listening  TRACK 8-9

While listening, check the items Richard and Susan decide to pack before **evacuating** their house.

| Guitar ☐ | Computer ☐ | Baby Blanket ☐ | Photo Album ☐ |
| Family Quilt ☐ | Family Pet ☐ | Jewelry Box ☐ | Important Documents ☐ |
| Trophy ☐ | Television ☐ | Medication ☐ | Hard Drive ☐ |

**evacuate** *(v.)*: to remove someone from a dangerous situation

## Post-listening

1. Which items did the family decide to take?
   • Did they leave right away?

2. Which items did they leave or forget?
   • What do you think will happen to the items they left?

3. Does it ever flood in your city?
   • Do you know anyone who has been affected by a flood?


What precautions could you take to avoid or prepare for the following emergencies? Choose from the list below and add your own recommendations.

- Earthquake
- Heart Attack
- Fire
- Flood
- Tsunami
- **Mugging**

- **Teach family members how to turn off gas, electricity, and water.**
- **Identify safe places in each room.**
- **Stick to well-lit and well-populated areas.**
- **Don't walk with your smart phone or wallet in your hand.**
- **Plan and practice an evacuation route.**
- **Keep important documents in a water tight bag or safe.**
- **Lower the amount of greasy and salty food you eat.**
- **Exercise often and reduce stress.**
- **Install smoke detectors in every room.**

**mug** *(v.)*: to rob someone on the street

# C. Well, You Really Should...

## Language Point: Strength of Advice or Commands

Mary thinks she is allergic to her lip gloss. What do you think she should do?

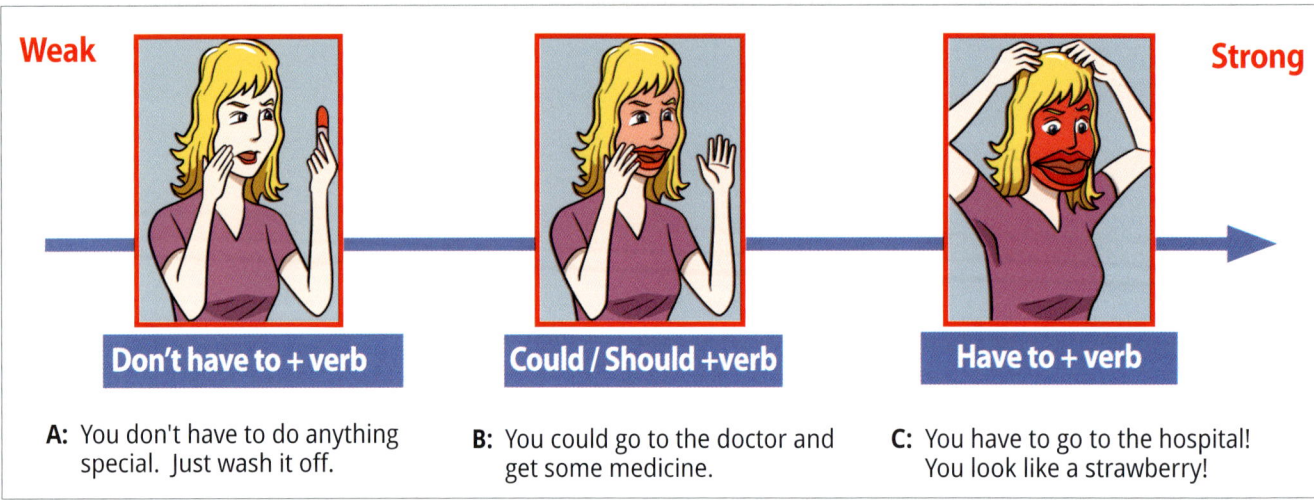

**A:** You don't have to do anything special. Just wash it off.

**B:** You could go to the doctor and get some medicine.

**C:** You have to go to the hospital! You look like a strawberry!

Below is a list of emergencies. Discuss what you think are good and bad ideas for each situation. Ask a follow-up question about the situation.

> **Example: Fire**
>
> **Good idea:** You could clear the area and look for a **fire extinguisher**. If you're in a tall building, you shouldn't use the elevator!
>
> **Bad idea:** You don't have to use the stairs. You should take time to gather all of your belongings – your laptop, your favorite dress, and your stamp collection!

| Situation | Good idea | Bad idea |
| --- | --- | --- |
| 1  Broken arm | | |
| 2  Hard drive crash | | |
| 3  **Pickpocketed** on vacation | | |
| 4  Bank robbery | | |
| 5  Allergic reaction | | |
| 6  Someone choking | | |
| 7  Stuck in the elevator | | |
| 8  Car breaks down | | |
| 9  Someone drowning | | |
| 10  Lost late at night | | |

**fire extinguisher** *(n.)*: a device used to stop a fire
**pickpocket** *(v.)*: to steal something from someone on the street

# Discussion Questions

1 When was the last time you had to deal with an emergency situation? Explain what happened.

2 Do you feel that it's safe to walk alone at night? Why or why not?

3 Are you the kind of person who can **keep cool** in an emergency, or do you panic?

4 Have you ever taken a first aid or lifesaving course?
   ▶ If so, what kind of techniques did you learn?
   ▶ Have you ever had to use them?

5 Is your house well protected in case of fire and robbery?
   ▶ What kinds of precautions have been taken?
   ▶ What kinds of precautions need to be taken?

6 Have you ever been mugged or pickpocketed?
   ▶ What happened?
   ▶ If not, do you know anyone who has?

7 Have you ever seen **an accident waiting to happen**?
   ▶ What was the situation?

8 Have you ever been in a scary situation while travelling?
   ▶ What happened?

**an accident waiting to happen** *(idiom)*: describes a situation that will most likely lead to a problem or accident
**keep cool** *(idiom)*: to remain calm

Unit 4 Better Safe Than Sorry | 69

# LESSON 2

## >> WARM UP

**Objectives:**
/ Expressing unexpected results

**A.**
1. What is the biggest problem facing your country today?
   > What could you do to fix this problem?
2. What is the biggest problem facing the world today?
   > What could you do to fix this problem?

**B. Rank the following problems in order from 1 (most serious) to 5 (least serious)**
   > Failing economy
   > Smoking
   > Pollution of the oceans
   > Typhoons
   > Terrorist attacks

# A. Expect the Unexpected

## Language Point: Expressing an Unexpected Result Using **Even Though** and **Although**

**Even though** and **Although** express something which is not expected.
- *Even though I'm on a diet, I ate an entire chocolate cake.*

◇ Note: Just like sentences with because and since, even though and although can come in the second part of a sentence.
*I ate an entire cake even though I'm on a diet.*

**PART 1** • Match the phrase on the left with its contrasting idea on the right using **even though** or **although**.

1. Jack studied hard
2. Susan went on a diet
3. Sometimes Lisa feels lonely
4. Grandpa is a **ladies' man**
5. Jack tried to impress his date
6. Richard didn't get the job
7. Mr. Squiggles is hungry

A. He has eaten three times today.
B. He was the most qualified.
C. He failed the exam.
D. She has a lot of friends.
E. She was not interested.
F. He has terrible **fashion sense**.
G. She still gained weight.

### Tip
In conversation it is common for speakers to end a sentence with the word **though**.

**A:** *The weather was cold yesterday.*
**B:** *Yes it was. I went to the beach though.*

**The meaning is:** Even though it was cold, I went to the beach.

**fashion sense** *(idiom)*: understanding of fashion trends
**ladies' man** *(n.)*: a man who attracts women

**PART 2** ● Use the given phrase and **even though** or **although** to express an unexpected result.

The temperature was about forty degrees.

**Example:**
- We waited in line for tickets **even though** the temperature was about forty degrees.
- **Although** the temperature was forty degrees, we went out for hot chocolate.

My friend loves smoking.

The weather man said it wouldn't rain.

The road looked safe.

That tiger looks friendly.

My cousin says he saw a U.F.O.

Nobody was hurt in the earthquake.

It's the middle of May.

There's a trash can in the parking lot.

The guide said the volcano was **dormant**.

**dormant** *(adj.)*: not active

# B. Saving the World, One Idea at a Time...

 • Comparatives

What are the good and bad points of each of the ideas below? Discuss the ideas and think of at least one good and bad point for each. Consider:
- Which option is more fun?
- Which option makes a person look better?
- Which option is better for people's health?
- Which option is better for the environment?

**PART 1**

## Consumerism

1. Buying a new car
   - Good point: New cars are comfortable and convenient.
   - Bad point: Driving a car creates pollution. Also, driving in traffic is stressful.
2. Buying new clothes
3. Drinking coffee from disposable cups
4. Buying a new notebook
5. Buying new shoes whenever a pair wears out
6. Taking a long shower with hot water every day
7. Buying new books
8. Getting fruit and vegetables from the grocery store
9. Buying a new smart phone whenever a new model is released

## Conservationism

1. Using public transportation
   - Good point: Public transportation makes less pollution than cars.
   - Bad point: Public transportation is crowded. Also, public transportation can be inconvenient if I miss a train or bus and arrive late to work.
2. Buying used clothes or trading clothes with friends
3. Drinking coffee from a reusable coffee cup
4. Making a notebook by stapling together recycled paper
5. Repairing an old pair of shoes
6. Taking a short shower every day
7. Going to the library
8. Growing your own fruits and vegetables
9. Using your smart phone until it breaks

**PART 2** Now, make sentences contrasting pairs of ideas. Use the good and bad points brainstormed above.

**Example:**
- *Although driving in traffic is stressful, cars are comfortable and convenient.*
- *Even though public transportation can be inconvenient, it is good for the environment because it makes less pollution than cars.*

**conservationism** *(n.)*: the idea that protecting the environment is beneficial
**consumerism** *(n.)*: belief in the idea that acquiring goods is positive and beneficial

# C. Doomsday, an Activity of Disastrous Proportions

**PART 1** ● Discuss the following ways the world might end. How likely is each one? Why do you think so?

**How will the world end?**

ASTEROID IMPACT

CLIMATE CHANGE

SUPER VIRUS

NUCLEAR WAR

MACHINES TAKE OVER

OTHER

**asteroid** *(n.)*: a rock that orbits around the sun
**take over** *(phrasal verb)*: to assume power over something

# PART 2 • The world has ended!

- There are only thirteen survivors on the entire planet, one of whom is an astronaut.
- The only way for the human race to continue is to leave Earth on a spaceship.
- The spaceship only fits six people.
- The astronaut must go.
- Of the remaining twelve people, only five can go.

## Which five of these people will continue the human race?

| | |
|---|---|
|  **Frank**<br>70 years old<br>Medical Doctor<br>Very **blunt** |  **Bonnie**<br>35 years old<br>Police Officer<br>Constant **hiccups** |
|  **Nicholas**<br>35 years old<br>Reformed Criminal<br>Amazing singer |  **Sophie**<br>31 years old<br>Lawyer<br>**Compulsive** liar |
|  **Eleanor**<br>43 years old<br>Scientist<br>**Scaredy cat** | 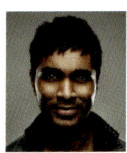 **Roberto**<br>30 years old<br>Farmer<br>Very quiet |
|  **Mark**<br>50 years old<br>Religious Leader<br>Perfect memory |  **Vinny**<br>33 years old<br>Construction Worker<br>Excellent with children |
|  **Luis**<br>55 years old<br>Electrician<br>Excellent writer |  **Anita**<br>27 years old<br>Medical Student<br>Forgetful |
|  **Gladys**<br>50 years old<br>Psychologist<br>Speaks six languages |  **Steve**<br>27 years old<br>Chef<br>Gambling addiction |

**blunt** *(adj.)*: extremely straightforward with one's words and actions
**compulsive** *(adj.)*: driven by strong drive to do certain things
**hiccups** *(n.)*: sound made that effects one's breathing
**scaredy cat** *(idiom)*: a person who is easily frightened or intimidated

- Likely possibilities
- Should and could for advice

### PART 3

After a long journey, the survivors of planet Earth land on their new home planet. You are the astronaut.

> The air is breathable.
> The temperature is very hot.
> The new planet has some plants and small trees, but there is no sign of intelligent life.

Using the people your group selected from Part 2, discuss how they could deal with the following situations.

1. The group needs a leader. Among the survivors from Part 2, who should they choose and why?
2. Several survivors are very depressed. Morale is very low. Nobody wants to do anything.
3. There is a fight between two of the crew members and they refuse to talk to one another.
    - Which two survivors do you think are most likely to get into a fight?
    - What can the group do to solve this problem?
4. The survivors do not want to spend more time inside the spaceship. They need to build shelter on the new planet.
5. There is a strange fungus growing on some of the important equipment. You're not sure if it's safe or dangerous.
    - One of the survivors tries to eat some of the strange fungus and gets very sick.
6. The survivors discover the planet is inhabited by small, furry, rabbit-like animals. What do you do with them?
7. The food supplies are slowly running out. There is a container full of various seeds, but the label is missing.
8. There is something wrong with the solar panels and they are not working well. You will need power if you want to keep using electronic devices.
9. Clothing is slowly wearing out.

Bonus: What are some other issues that you will need to solve in order to continue the human race? What are some possible solutions?

# Discussion Questions

1. What is important to do and **watch out** for during or after the following natural disasters:
   - An earthquake?
   - A forest fire?
   - A tsunami?
   - A **tornado**?
   - An avalanche?
   - A **drought**?
   - An **outbreak**?

2. Do you prefer to live carefully, or to **take risks**?
   - Why is it **better to be safe than sorry**?

3. There are some ongoing issues happening in our world every day, such as starvation, poverty, and war.
   - Would you consider these issues to be emergencies? Why or why not?

4. What are some examples of manmade disasters?
   - What could be done to fix these problems?

5. What are some ways we can **reach out** to people who have been affected by disasters?

6. What disasters are possible in your country? Do these things ever worry you?

## UNIT 4 REVIEW

**How well can you use:**
- ☐ Language to express different levels of importance?
- ☐ Even though and although to express unexpected results?

What do you need to study more?

---

**better to be safe than sorry** *(idiom)*: the idea that one should always try to be careful
**drought** *(n.)*: a period of water shortage
**outbreak** *(n.)*: the sudden spread of something such as sickness or conflict
**reach out** *(phrasal verb)*: help someone in need
**take a risk** *(idiom)*: to do something without knowing what the result will be
**tornado** *(n.)*: air that moves over land and leaves destruction on the land that it touches
**watch out** *(phrasal verb)*: to be alert to a problem or danger

# Activity: Create a Superhero

Work with a partner to create a superhero that can solve what you consider to be the most urgent problems in the world today.

**Example:**

**Superhero's name:** Woof Woman

**Problem that he or she wants to solve:** *Woof Woman wants to save dogs that live on the streets without a home.*

**Appearance and costume:** *Woof Woman wears all black with stylish accessories (such as a hat, necklace, and sunglasses).*

**Superpower:** *Woof Woman has a cell phone that barks whenever a dog in distress is nearby. Her cell phone can also communicate with dogs, so dogs can send her text messages expressing their thoughts.*

**Sidekick:** *Woof Woman is never seen without her trusty dog, Hubert, by her side.*

**Enemy:** *Woof Woman's enemies are thoughtless dog owners everywhere.*

### PART 1

| | |
|---|---|
| **Superhero's name:** | |
| **Problem that he or she wants to solve:** | |
| **Appearance and costume:** | |
| **Superpower:** | |
| **Sidekick:** | |
| **Enemy:** | |

### PART 2

What would your superhero do if he or she had to face their enemy?

**Example:** *Woof Woman would talk to thoughtless dog owners about caring for their pets. She would also use her cell phone to share mistreated dogs' opinions about their owners.*

What does your superhero do in his or her free time?

**Example:** *Woof Woman likes to shop for dog treats and sit at outdoor café tables with Hubert.*

**sidekick (n.):** a hero's assistant

# The Flood: Moving Forward

By **Leigh King**, PNN

The past several weeks of wet weather have finally taken a toll as a flood submerged the local area last night, leaving two meters of water covering some roads, and leaving residents stranded, unable to return to their homes.

Meteorologists said that the sudden flood was caused by heavy rain even though the spring season is usually dry in this area. Stan Holmes, a local weather man, said, "Such a large amount of rain is unusual for this time of year. We were all surprised that the rain continued for two whole weeks. Hopefully now we'll have sunny weather for the rest of the spring."

The flood has touched many people, some in tragic ways.

"This flood was completely unexpected," said local resident Richard Thompson, "we barely had enough time to grab our most valued possessions before the water began to cover our floors in the house. Although we managed to save our important possessions, we were in such a hurry that we forgot to bring our family cat, Mr. Squiggles, out of the house. Now, we're not sure where he is."

As the families affected by the flood begin to repair their homes and move forward with their lives, they have asked for the support of the local community.

Police deputy Darren Deeds told PNN that although the flooding was sudden, there were no reports of casualties or injuries. "Everyone was able to get out of the neighborhood in an orderly fashion. Being prepared for these kinds of emergencies is the most important thing. I did see the strangest thing, though," Deeds said, "It was a cat floating down the street on a wooden door. He must be well out to sea now."

## A. Discussion

1. What caused the flood?
   ▶ Why was the flood unexpected?
2. What kinds of problems do you think that a flood might cause for a community?
   ▶ How can these problems be solved?
3. How can people help each other during or after an emergency such as a fire or flood?

## B. Writing

Write a short emergency plan for evacuating your house in case of an emergency such as a flood. Think about:
▶ What will you do before the emergency to prepare?
▶ What steps are important to take during an emergency to be safe?
▶ What will you have to do after the emergency is over?

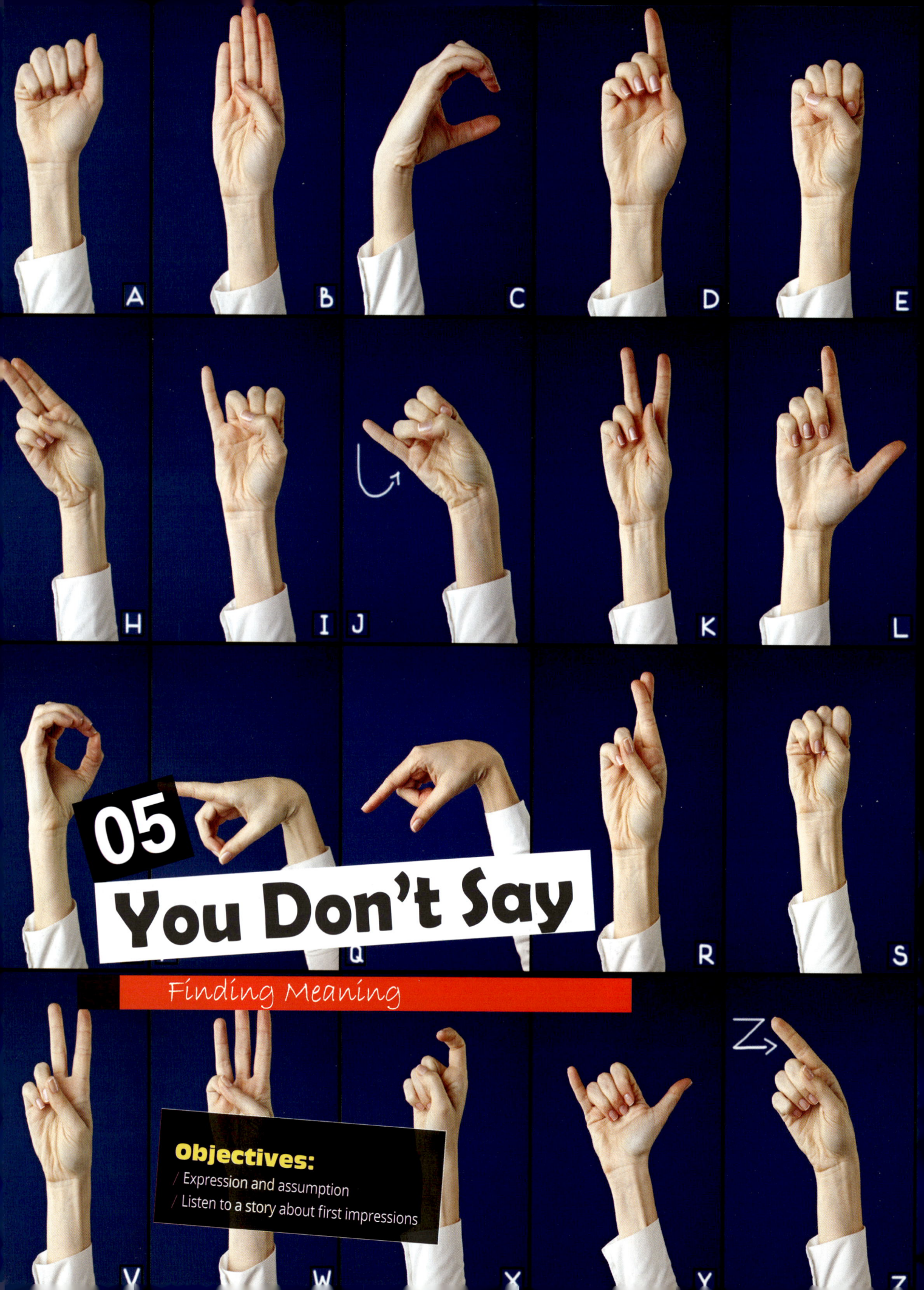

# 05 You Don't Say

*Finding Meaning*

**Objectives:**
/ Expression and assumption
/ Listen to a story about first impressions

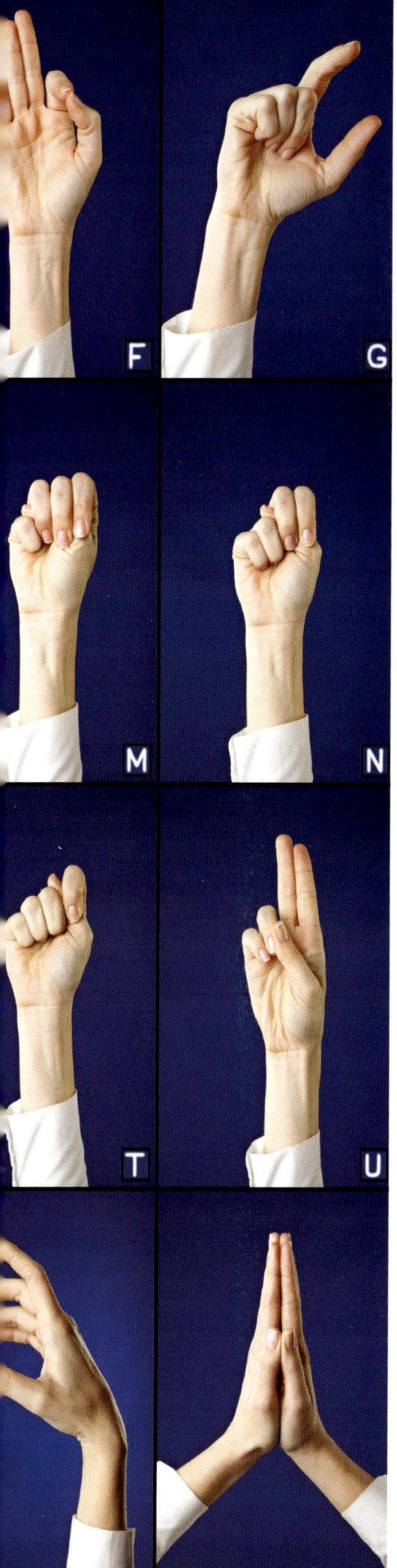

# WARM UP

**How do you express the following phrases without speaking?**

- I don't know.
- Call me.
- It's too loud in here.
- Please sit down.
- I'm thinking.
- I'm scared!
- Follow me.
- Looks delicious.
- You're late.
- I'm tired.
- Great job.
- You're cute.

## IDIOMS

- **Poker face**
  No one can see when she's lying because she has an excellent *poker face*.
- **Jump to conclusions**
  I wouldn't *jump to any conclusions* about him just because he doesn't care about fashion.

## PHRASAL VERBS

- **Figure out**
  The best way to *figure out* a word you don't know is to explain its use, location, and description to the person you are asking.
- **Get across**
  Sometimes it's difficult to *get your meaning across* with just words.

## COLLOCATIONS

- **To make eye contact**
  It is important to *make eye contact* with the interviewer during a job interview.
- **Pass judgment**
  It's not fair to *pass judgment* on her just because of how she looks.

Unit 5 You Don't Say | 81

# LESSON 1

## A. Body Language

## PART 1

Discuss what the people are trying to say in each picture and match them with the expressions below. Then discuss when and where you would use the expression.

1. Putting your hand on your forehead
2. Bowing
3. Holding your nose
4. A short hug and sometimes a kiss on the cheek
5. Smiling with your eyes closed
6. Putting your hand in front of you, palm out
7. Bending forward, holding your hands to your stomach
8. Rolling your eyes
9. Putting your hand to your chin
10. Pointing in a direction

a. I'm thinking.
b. Hello. *(informal)*
c. I am content.
d. Something smells bad.
e. I am in pain!
f. Look at that!
g. Nice to meet you. *(formal)*
h. I made a mistake.
i. Stop right there!
j. I'm really not interested in what you're saying.

Unit 5 You Don't Say | 83

**Talking to a coworker**

**Taking an evening class**  **On a date together**

**PART 2** ● Now consider yourself in each of the above situations.
- How do you act and present yourself?
- What do you think your choices say to others?
- Do you think this a bad or good thing?

## PART 1

Discuss what the people are trying to say in each picture and match them with the expressions below. Then discuss when and where you would use the expression.

1. Putting your hand on your forehead
2. Bowing
3. Holding your nose
4. A short hug and sometimes a kiss on the cheek
5. Smiling with your eyes closed
6. Putting your hand in front of you, palm out
7. Bending forward, holding your hands to your stomach
8. Rolling your eyes
9. Putting your hand to your chin
10. Pointing in a direction

a. I'm thinking.
b. Hello. *(informal)*
c. I am content.
d. Something smells bad.
e. I am in pain!
f. Look at that!
g. Nice to meet you. *(formal)*
h. I made a mistake.
i. Stop right there!
j. I'm really not interested in what you're saying.

Unit 5 You Don't Say | 83

# B. It's Show Time!

## Language Point : Making Assumptions

**Seems/Looks + adjective** expresses opinions about something based on appearance.
- He looks nice because he's wearing a bright-colored shirt and smiling.
- She seems friendly because she's talking to lots of people.

**Seems like/Looks like + noun** makes an assumption about something based on appearance.
- He looks like the kind of person who cares about his health.
- She seemed like she was lonely when we saw her walking in the park the other day.

## Pre-listening

Look at the pictures. Describe how each person looks or seems based on his or her appearance.

## Listening  TRACK 10-11

Which of the television programs below did Lisa and Richard see as they were flipping through the channels? Circle the shows that Lisa and Richard talk about. Put a star next to the show that they decided to watch.

## Post-listening

1. After listening to Richard and Lisa's conversation, do you feel like your **first impressions** of the people in the pictures were correct?
   - How do the people in the pictures look or seem now that you know a bit more about them?
2. Is it fair to judge people based on your first impression?
   - Do you consider yourself a **good judge of character**?

**first impression** *(idiom)*: the initial opinion of someone
**good judge of character** *(idiom)*: able to decide whether someone is good or bad easily

# C. The Power of First Impressions

**PART 1** ● Discuss what impression Blake and Zoey make based on their appearance, behavior, and choices.

 **Blake** looks friendly because he has a big smile. He looks like a relaxed person because his hair is a bit messy.

 **Zoey** seems like a very serious person because she's not smiling. She looks like a creative person because her hair has an unusual style.

## This is them.

① Getting dressed in the morning for work

② Driving to work

③ Eating lunch

## Talking to a coworker

## Taking an evening class

## On a date together

**PART 2** • Now consider yourself in each of the above situations.
- How do you act and present yourself?
- What do you think your choices say to others?
- Do you think this a bad or good thing?

# Discussion Questions

1 Why do you think we use body language to communicate?
   ▶ If people did not use body language, how would this affect communication?

2 A friend of yours from another country is coming to visit you. What kind of body language should they not use in your country?

3 How important is it to understand the gestures and body language of other cultures?
   ▶ How has body language helped you while traveling in other countries?

4 Is it important to make eye contact with someone when speaking?
   ▶ What kind of judgment would you pass on someone who uses too much eye contact?

5 Do you use your hands to gesture while you are speaking?
   ▶ What miscommunications can happen when not using body language?

6 Do you **jump to conclusions** based on how someone is dressed?
   ▶ How important is our choice of clothing and accessories to how other people see us?

7 How does the face you show the world affect your chances of success?
   ▶ Is it more important to show the world you are a happy or serious person?

8 What kind of body language indicates that a person is lying?
   ▶ Do you have a good **poker face**?

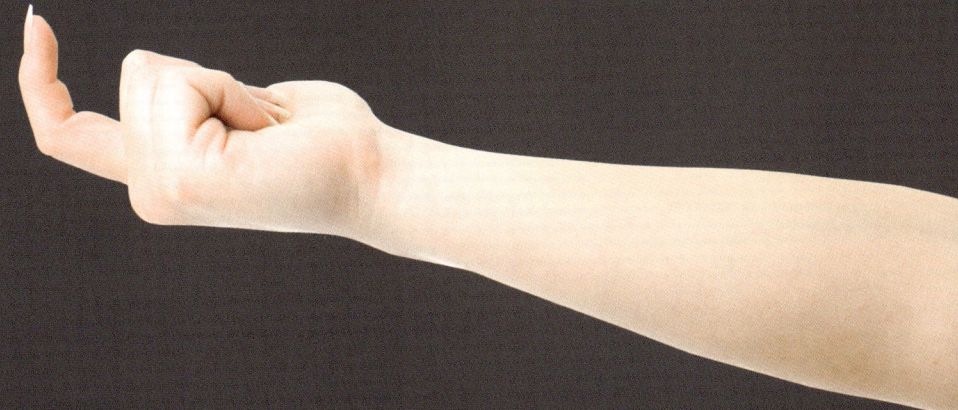

**jump to conclusions** *(idiom)*: to make a quick decision
**poker face** *(idiom)*: a face that expresses no emotion

# LESSON 2

## >> WARM UP

**Objectives:**
/ Describing what kind or which one

**A.** If you don't know a vocabulary word in English, what is the best way to find out its meaning?

**B.** Below are sections of larger photographs. Decide what the thing in the picture is.
- What purpose(s) does it have?
- Where is it found?
- What does it look like?

# A. It's a Thing-a-ma-bob.

- Using because and since
- Comparatives

**A:** *She's so cute!*
**B:** *Which one?*
**A:** *The girl who is wearing the red dress and the black hat.*
**B:** *They're both wearing a red dress and a black hat.*
**A:** *The girl that's on the left.*
**B:** *I disagree. The girl that's on the right is cuter.*

## Language Point : Describing "What Kind" or "Which One"

**Who**, **Which**, and **That** are relative pronouns that can be used to give more information about a non-specific noun.

**Who or That**- is used to describe or define a person.
- *I met a man. What kind of man was he?*
- *I met a man **who** plays the flute. I met a man **that** likes kittens.*

**Which or That**- is used to describe or define a thing.
- *The man had a flute **which** he played when he walked.*
- *It was a magic flute **that** made kittens follow him around.*

**PART 1** ● Read the sentences and ask the question. Use **"the"** to make the general noun specific and use **"who, which, or that"** to describe it. Then ask your partner(s) their opinion.

### Example:
One day is hot and sunny. Another day is cool and rainy.
- Which day do you prefer? Why?
   *I prefer **the** day **that** is cool and rainy because I really hate sweating. How about you?*

1. One student studied until 4 a.m. Another student went to bed at 11 p.m.
   ▶ Who did better on the test? Why?
2. One car is very fast and expensive. Another car uses very little gas and is also expensive.
   ▶ Which car would you choose? Why?
3. One restaurant across the street sells greasy burgers and soda. Another restaurant across the street sells salads and fruit juice.
   ▶ Which restaurant is better? Why?
4. Movie A has a lot of blood and violence. Movie B has a lot of kissing and talking.
   ▶ Which movie is more entertaining? Why?
5. One city has a lot of beautiful old buildings, museums, and rainy weather. Another city has great food, shopping, and really hot weather.
   ▶ Which is better for a vacation? Why?
6. A woman who has a very stressful job spent the weekend sleeping. Another woman who has a very stressful job spent the weekend enjoying her hobbies.
   ▶ Who felt more relaxed after the weekend? Why?

### PART 2

Choose a person and describe their profession using *who* or *that*. Guess who it is by the clues given and ask a follow up question about the person's job.

> **Example:**
> **A:** *This is someone who wears big shoes, a red nose, and makes children laugh.*
> **B:** *You're thinking about a clown. Do you like clowns?*
> **A:** *Actually, I find them terrifying.*

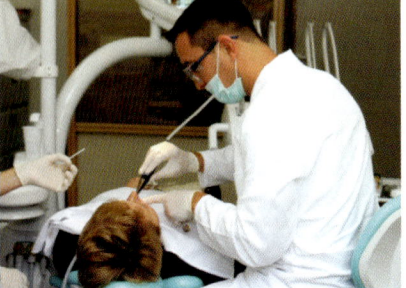

## B. Forbidden Words

**CAUTION**
- Try to get your partner to guess the words/phrases pictured below.
- DO NOT say any of the forbidden words.
- Also, do not use any proper nouns (names of companies, people, holidays or places) in your descriptions.

**Example:**
A: *This is a thing that you have around 1 P.M. to give you energy.*
B: *Coffee?*
A: *No, not coffee. This is a thing that is similar to dinner or breakfast.*
B: *Oh, I know! Lunch!*
A: *Yes, lunch is correct.*

## STUDENT A

### Lunch

**Forbidden:** eat, meal, afternoon

### Air Conditioner

**Forbidden:** summer, cool, classroom, heater

### Tape

**Forbidden:** stick, plastic, clear, office

### Coffee

**Forbidden:** drink, café, brown, bean

### Spaceship

**Forbidden:** outer space, rocket

### Song
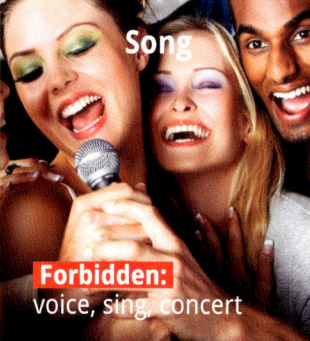
**Forbidden:** voice, sing, concert

### Joy

**Forbidden:** happy, feeling, smile

### Tennis Racket

**Forbidden:** tennis, sport, play

### Puppy

**Forbidden:** baby, dog, small

### Flower

**Forbidden:** plant, pretty, grow

### Wheel

**Forbidden:** circle, bike, car, spin

### Music

**Forbidden:** listen, hear, notes, play

# CAUTION

- Try to get your partner to guess the words/phrases pictured below.
- DO NOT say any of the forbidden words.
- Also, do not use any proper nouns (names of companies, people, holidays or places) in your descriptions.

**Example:**
**B:** *This is a thing that you might do when you're bored. You wear sneakers to do this.*
**A:** *Hmmm...walking?*
**B:** *No...this is a thing that you do in a gym. You use something that is orange and black to do this.*
**A:** *Oh! Basketball!*
**B:** *That's right!*

# STUDENT B

**Basketball**
Forbidden: ball, play, sport, athlete

**Star**
Forbidden: sky, night, bright, sun

**Gum**
Forbidden: chew, candy

**Truck**
Forbidden: drive, road, dump

**Map**
Forbidden: guide, find, lost, tourist

**Math**
Forbidden: calculator, number, school, test

**Plate**
Forbidden: eat, meal, dish, food

**Dance**
Forbidden: move, music, hip hop, ballet

**Strawberry**
Forbidden: fruit, eat, red, sweet

**Sky**
Forbidden: blue, cloud, sun

**Love**
Forbidden: feeling, romantic, boyfriend, girlfriend

**Party**
Forbidden: celebrate, music, dance

# CAUTION

- Try to get your partner to guess the words/phrases pictured below.
- DO NOT say any of the forbidden words.
- Also, do not use any proper nouns (names of companies, people, holidays or places) in your descriptions.

**Example:**
**C:** *This is a thing that you might do when you're bored. You do this with your eyes.*
**B:** *Watching a movie?*
**C:** *No. This is something sort of like that, but you do this at home.*
**B:** *Watching television!*
**C:** *Right! Television is the answer!*

# STUDENT C

### Television

**Forbidden:** remote, watch, program, show

### Coat

**Forbidden:** warm, winter, jacket, clothing

### Motorcycle

**Forbidden:** ride, wheel

### Sneaker

**Forbidden:** sport, run, basketball

### Subway

**Forbidden:** transportation, public, underground

### Jeans

**Forbidden:** pants, clothing, denim, blue

### Movie

**Forbidden:** watch, theater, actor, popcorn

### Computer
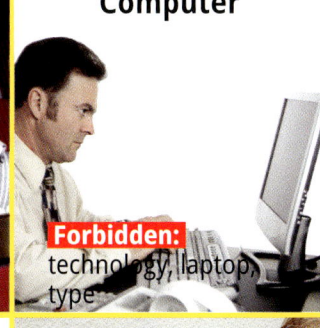
**Forbidden:** technology, laptop, type

### Winter

**Forbidden:** cold, snow, ice, season

### Sock

**Forbidden:** shoe, foot, warm, wear

### Book

**Forbidden:** read, paper, study, school

### Video Game

**Forbidden:** play, television, character

# C. Hello, My Name is Dave.

You are a judge at the…

19th Annual
Dave Convention

…and every Dave is invited.

**PART 1** •

As the judge, choose the recipient for the following Dave Awards and explain your decision:

### MOST AND LEAST / BEST AND WORST

☆ Most and Least Exciting
☆ Most and Least **Reliable**
☆ Most and Least Professional
☆ Best Dave
☆ Worst Dave
☆ Dave You Would Most Likely…

-Want to Be Friends With
-Ask for Help
-Avoid Talking to on the Street
-Hire for Your Company

Make Up Your Own Awards:
1._____
2._____

**Example:**
**A:** *I think the award for the most lazy Dave should go to the Dave who is yawning.*
**B:** *I disagree. I think it should go to the Dave that is not wearing a shirt. He was too lazy to put one on!*

---

**reliable** *(adj.)*: someone or something that is there when you need it

94 | SLE Generations 2B

**PART 2** ● **These Are the Daves I Know**

**Step 1**  Choose a Dave from the previous page, but don't tell anyone who you chose.

**Step 2**  Take turns asking each other questions in order to find out which Dave everyone chose. You should answer your questions as if you were that Dave. You will have twenty seconds before you must switch to questioning another Dave.

> **Student A:** *Hello, Dave.*
> **Student B:** *Hi, Dave. So, do you enjoy playing sports?*
> **Student A:** *Not really, Dave. Sports are a lot of work.*
> **Student B:** *Really?*
> **Student A:** *Yeah, I prefer relaxing. Do you like movies?*
> **Student B:** *I guess so. As long as they're not too scary.*
>
> **SWITCH!**
>
> **Student B:** *Hey, Dave! What is your favorite hobby?*
> **Student C:** *I really like walking in the woods…*

**Step 3**  After several minutes, come back together as a class and guess which Dave each person was.

> **Student A:** *He seemed really lazy.*
> **Student C:** *I agree. He didn't want to do anything!*
> **Student A:** *I think is he the Dave that is yawning on the stage.*
> **Student B:** *That's right! I am!*

**Alternate rule:** Write down a Dave on a small piece of paper and hand it to someone else in the class. That person cannot look at who they are, but everyone else should be able to see the name on the paper. Then ask that person questions based on the piece of paper until that person figures out who they are.

# Discussion Questions

**1** Have you ever been in a situation when you couldn't remember the word for what you wanted to say?
- ▶ How did you resolve the situation?
- ▶ How do you **get your meaning across** if you don't know how to say something in English?

**2** How can you **figure out** a vocabulary word without using a dictionary?
- ▶ Can you describe something's location, use, and appearance?

**3** How important is it to know a lot of vocabulary when communicating with a native speaker of another language?
- ▶ Why do you think so?

**4** What kind of people bother you?
- ▶ What are your pet peeves? *I am bothered by people who….*

**5** What is an ideal friend like? *An ideal friend is someone who……….*

**6** What kind of movies do you like? *I like movies that…….*

**7** What would your dream job be? *I want a job that……*

**8** What is the best kind of vacation? *I like vacations that……*

## UNIT 5 REVIEW

**How well can you use:**
- ☐ Language to correct information?
- ☐ Who, which or that to describe or define things and people?

What do you need to study more?

**figure out** *(phrasal verb)*: to make sense of, to resolve
**get across** *(phrasal verb)*: to communicate or express information

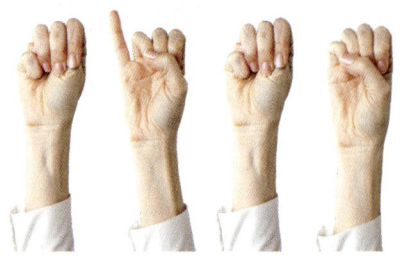

# Activity: Charades

1 Below is a list of categories. Work with your whole class to create a gesture for each category.
2 Choose a category and mime the gesture for that category.
3 Think of a word or phrase related to that category that you can mime. There are a few examples below.
4 Mime the word or phrase that you chose until someone in the class says the word.
  • Optional: To give an extra clue, hold up a finger for every word you are miming.
5 Whoever says your word repeats steps 2-4 with his or her own word or phrase!
  The student who guesses the most words by the end of the game wins!

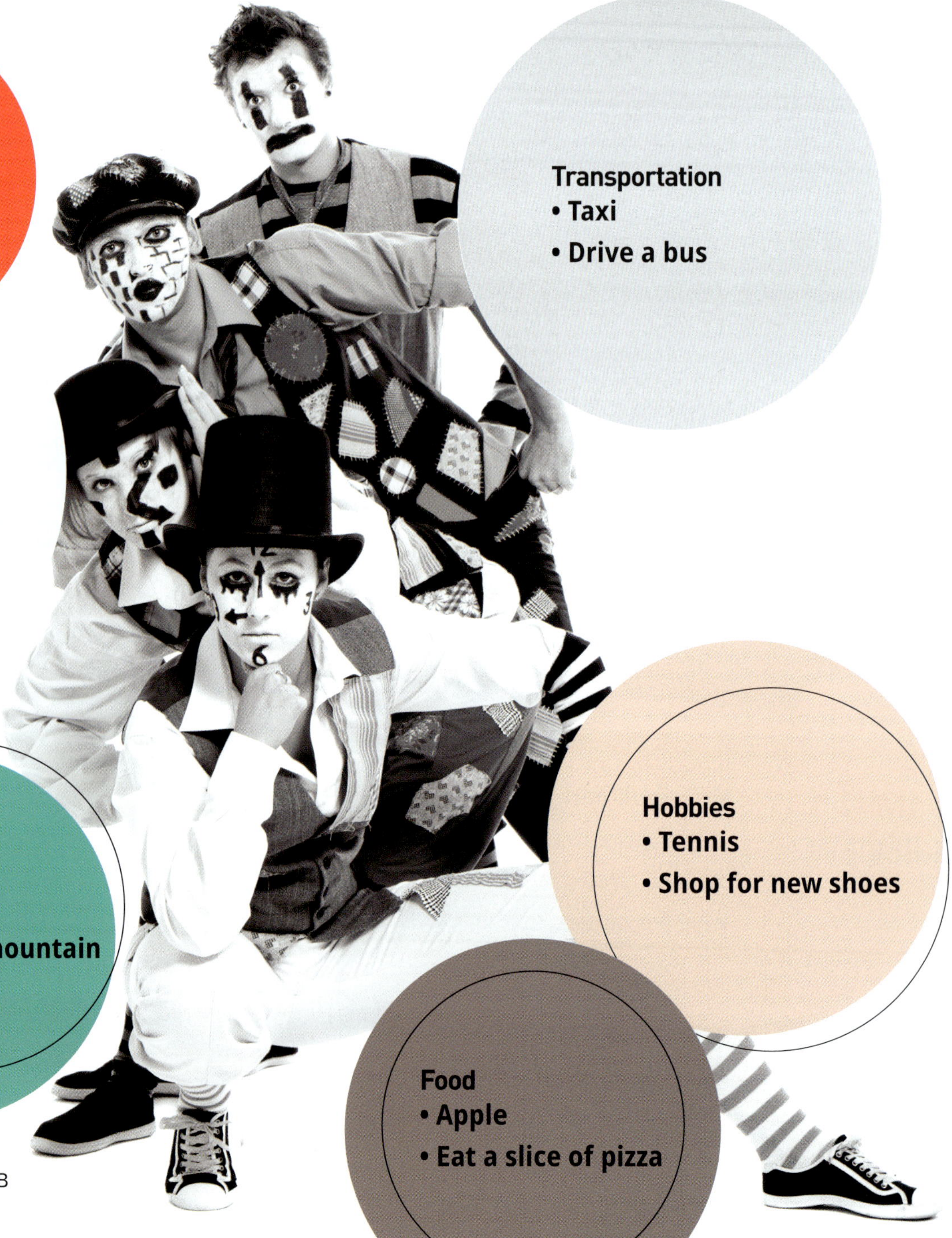

**Animals**
• Cat
• Ride a horse

**Transportation**
• Taxi
• Drive a bus

**Movies**
• Popcorn
• Watch a sad movie

**Travel**
• Souvenir
• Climb a mountain

**Hobbies**
• Tennis
• Shop for new shoes

**Food**
• Apple
• Eat a slice of pizza

# Segue

**channel 35**
## Happy Family 8 p.m.
Follow Steve and Janet Smith and their three children through the ups and downs of life in this popular family drama. In tonight's episode, Steve, who is a doctor, will deal with the challenges of Take Your Child to Work Day. His 10-year-old daughter, Annie, will accompany him to the hospital. Annie, who hopes to become a doctor someday, will befriend a patient and learn some valuable lessons about life, medicine, and her father's love.

**channel 32**
## Daily Gag Report 8 p.m.
The top news of the day, presented by hit comedian Joey Jokeson and his cast. Tonight's episode will include interviews with people who own successful cafes, as well as a musical performance by hit band, the Crimson Kings.

**channel 38**
## Socal Life 8 p.m.
Life is never boring in the city of Socal! Watch the real-life adventures of a group of high school students. In tonight's episode, Farah, who is planning the high school's Spring Sunny Dance, will struggle to balance planning the dance, finding the perfect dress, and finding a date to the event. Farah's friend Natalia, who is a member of the school orchestra, will try to help Farah do it all.

**channel 47**
## Cool Science 8 p.m.
Science for people who live in the real world! Tonight, Scientist James Block, a Jacobson Research Fellow from Smithson University presents his current research into safe car technology and the effect that it will have on your life. Learn valuable tips about how to make your current car safer.

**channel 50**
## Law and Justice 8 p.m.
Follow detectives from the Songtown crime lab as they investigate local incidents in this hit crime drama. This evening's episode will follow the detective team as they search for Sandra Patel, a famous artist who was about to unveil an exhibit of paintings at the museum. Detective Gomez, who is preparing to retire from her job with the team, will begin to say goodbye and remember her time working in Songtown.

## A. Discussion
1. Which of the television shows on this page would you most likely watch? Why?
   ▶ Which of the television shows on this page would you least likely watch?
2. What kinds of shows do you prefer to watch?

## B. Writing
Write a summary like those above describing an episode of your favorite television show.

Unit 5 You Don't Say | 99

# 06
# Coulda, Woulda, Shoulda

## Past Speculations and Regrets

**Objectives:**
/ Speculate about the past
/ Listen to a story about travel

## WARM UP

What happened in the picture?
Was his team winning or losing?
How do you know?

### IDIOMS

- **What's done is done.**
  I would like to go back to college and change my major, but *what's done is done*.
- **Hindsight is 20/20.**
  I wish I hadn't quit my last job. It was better than the job I have now. I guess *hindsight is 20/20*.

### PHRASAL VERBS

- **Look back on**
  When I get older, I'll probably *look back on* this time as the best of my life.
- **Chew over**
  I shouldn't spend so much time *chewing over* my mistake. I can't change what I've done.

### COLLOCATIONS

- **No regrets**
  I have *no regrets* about my time living abroad.
- **Guess about**
  I can only make a *guess about* what happened to my car. I parked it right here.

Unit 6  Coulda, Woulda, Shoulda  |  **101**

# LESSON 1

## A. Who Stole the Cookie from the Cookie Jar?

**Language Point : Speculate About the Past**

LESS CERTAIN

MORE CERTAIN

Who stole the cookie from the cookie jar?

**Positive:**   **Might/Could** + have + past participle
*Jack could have eaten the cookies.*

**Must** + have + past participle
*Jack must have eaten the cookies.*

**Negative:**   **Might not** + have + past participle
*Jack might not have eaten the cookies.*

**Must not/ Could not** + have + past participle
*Jack couldn't have eaten the cookies.*

**speculate** *(v.)*: to make a guess about something

Look at the pictures below and answer the questions with a guess. Give a reason why you think so.

> **Example:**
> Charles and Martha are not talking with each other.
> **A:** *They **might have had** an argument about what to do on vacation.*
> ▶ They are standing in a long line to get into a restaurant.
> **B:** *Charles **must have** forgotten to make a reservation!*

### 1. Richard and Susan on a cruise
- Where did the cruise go?
- Did anything go wrong?
- The cruise had many activities including diving, water skiing, gambling, and ballroom dancing. Which activities did they enjoy?
- Susan said she wanted to do something exciting. What did they try?
- They stopped on an island to sightsee. What did they forget to do?
- Where did they get the **lifeboat**?
- How long were they out to sea?

### 2. Lisa and Biff on vacation
- Where in the world were they?
- What were they looking for?
- What activities did they enjoy?
- Could they speak the language?
- How was the weather?
- Did they go out to a fancy dinner?
- Did they enjoy the food on vacation?

### 3. Jack on a date
- What kind of restaurant did he meet his date at?
- What food did they order?
- Was he late? Why?
- She got angry with him after he said he had a meeting. Where was he?
- Jack gave her flowers and she started crying. Why?
- He told her she looked "interesting" in her outfit. How did she react?
- She said she was going to the restroom and didn't return. Where did she go?

**lifeboat** *(n.)*: a small boat that is kept on a larger boat in case of emergencies

# B. Squiggles' Quest

## Pre-listening

Mr. Squiggles has been missing ever since the flood! Look at the map and guess where Mr. Squiggles might have gone by matching each photo to a location on the map.

## Listening  TRACK 12-13

Now listen to the dialogue and find out where Mr. Squiggles went.

## Post-listening

Choose a place that you have been to or a place you want to visit. Your partner needs to ask yes/no questions to figure out which place you've selected.

### Example:

**A:** *Is this a place that is cold?*

**B:** *Actually, no. This is a place that is very warm.*

**A:** *Are there deserts there?*

**B:** *Lots of them.*

**A:** *You **might have gone** to Egypt.*

**B:** *Yes!*

**A:** *Wow, really, have you been to Egypt?*

**B:** *Yes, when I was a teenager, I...*

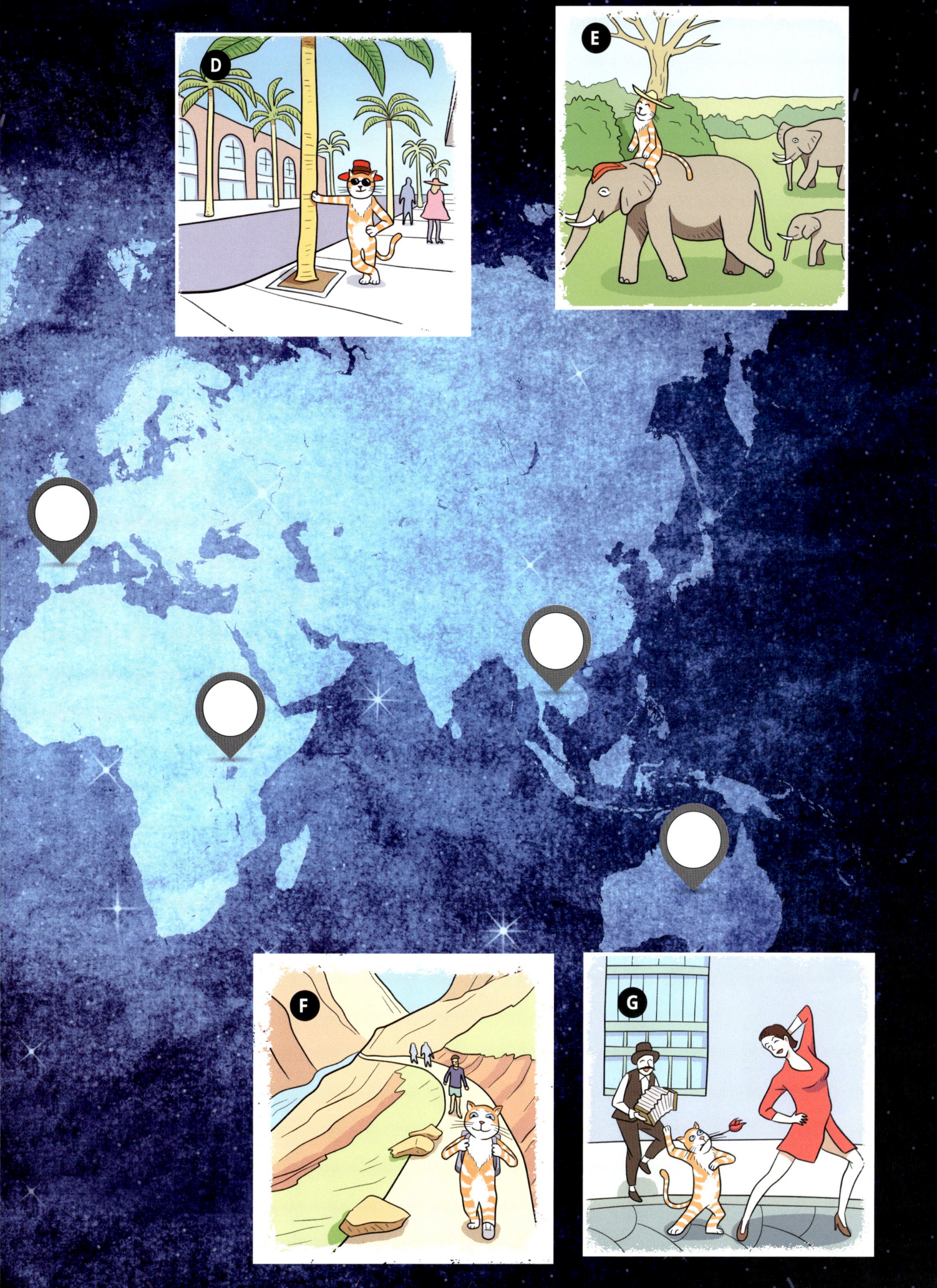

### Post-listening

Based on what you see in the following suitcases:
Where do you think the owner went?
What did they do there?
Why do you think so?

# C. The Graphs of Life

- Giving reasons with because and since

**PART 1** ● Based on the information given in the graphs below, speculate about what could have happened to James and Sue on their blind date.

### James and Sue's Blind Date

James and Sue went on a blind date. They met at a restaurant at 7 P.M.
Based on their feelings, try to decide what might have happened during the date.

> **A:** *James might have been disappointed at the beginning of the date because Sue was late. She must have looked beautiful, though, because James was ecstatic when he met her.*
>
> **B:** *Sue was happy at the beginning of the date. She could have started to feel unhappy when she met him because he didn't bring any flowers.*

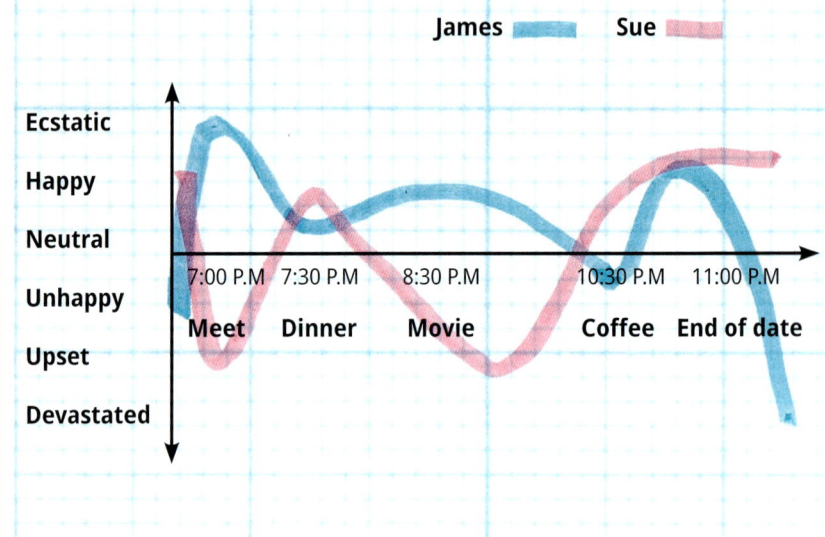

### Alex's Life

Alex was 20 years old in the year 2000.

Based on the feelings shown in the graph, try to decide when the life events in the box might have occurred.

**Life Events**
- Get a new job
- Fail an important test
- Break up with a girlfriend
- Discover a new hobby
- Move to a new city
- Get married
- Make a mistake
- Lose something important

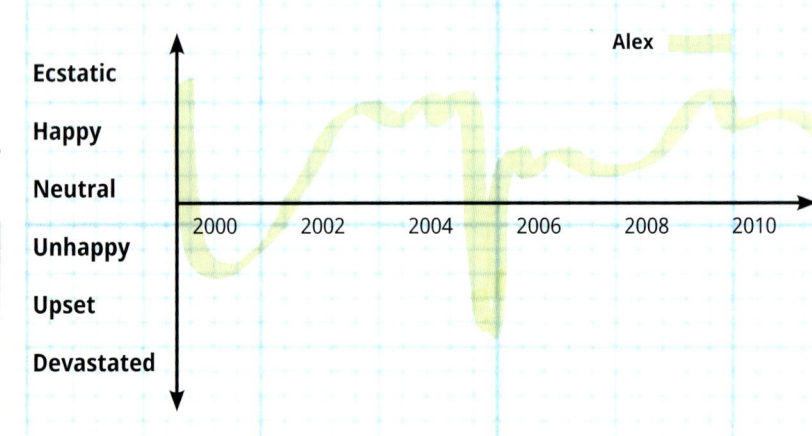

**PART 2** ●

Make a graph of the last 5 years of your own life. Trade graphs with your partner and speculate about what happened in each of your lives.

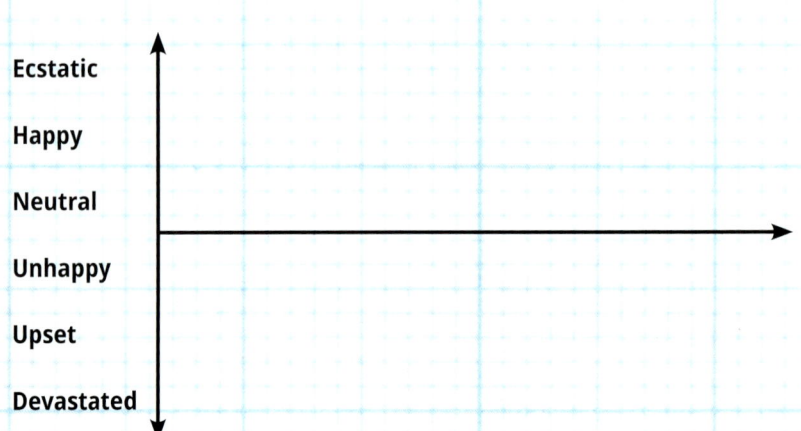

108 | SLE Generations 2B

# Discussion Questions

1. Do you like TV shows that are about unsolved mysteries?
   - ▶ Do you think you would be a good detective? Why or Why not?
   - ▶ Does your country have any famous mysteries? What do you think happened?

2. Has anything ever **slipped your mind**?
   - ▶ What do you think might have happened?

3. Can you make some guesses about what your SLE instructor was like in high school?

4. Have you ever lost something and not been able to find it?
   - ▶ What do you think might have happened to it?

5. What do you think the rest of your classmates did last weekend?
   - ▶ Why do you think they enjoy these things?

6. Why has English become one the most widely spoken languages in the world?

7. Can you recall any strange or unexplained events in your life?
   - ▶ What do you think the explanation might be?

**slip one's mind** *(idiom)*: to forget about something

# LESSON 2

## >> WARM UP

**Objectives:**
/ Express regrets

**What do you wish was different about…**
…public transportation?
…education?
…your city?
…your country?

# A. Coulda, Shoulda, Woulda but Didn't.

## Language Point: Expressing Regret and Advice in the Past

**Should + Have + Past Participle** expresses...

... regret about something you did.
- I **should've brought** an umbrella.
- I **shouldn't have** said that. I think I gave away the surprise.

...or advice about something a person did or did not do (**hindsight** advice).
- He **shouldn't have said** that. She looks angry with him.

**Could + Have + Past Participle** expresses choices that were not made.
- You **could've bought** an umbrella at the subway station or **borrowed** one from your coworker.
- ◇ Note: Could have is not used in the negative to express regret.

Look at the pictures below and think about what things the person(s) **shouldn't have done** and what they **could have done** differently.

**Example:** Randall

**A:** *He shouldn't have gotten a tattoo! He's too young.*

**B:** *He could have waited until he was older. His mom is going to kill him.*

**C:** *He could have just sent some flowers to the girl he wants to impress.*

**Darla**

**Reggie**

**Agatha and Angie**

**Penny**

**Bonny and Clyde**

**hindsight** *(n.)*: the understanding gained after an incident has occurred

# B. Life Coach

## PART 1

> Imagine that you are in one of the situations below.
> Ask your partner what you could have or should have done differently.
> Give advice on what your partner should have done and what they could do in the future.

• Giving advice with could and should

**Example:**

**A:** *I got into a big argument with my coworker. After the argument, I found out that she's been really sick recently. I feel terrible! What **could I have done** differently?*

**B:** *You **shouldn't have gotten** into an argument so quickly. You could try to talk to her about what is bothering you.*

---

- Your boyfriend or girlfriend went away to military service.
- Now, you don't know if you can wait for him or her to come back.

---

- You bought a used computer one month ago from a friend for $1000.
- A month after you bought the computer, it stopped working.
- The computer needs $1000 worth of repairs.

---

- You are working on a project with your friend.
- You've been so busy that you haven't even started it yet.
- Your friend is upset because she had to work all night to finish the project alone.

---

- Your best friend has a terrible voice but thinks his voice is fantastic.
- When he asked about it, you told him his voice was "unique".
- Lately, he has been talking about trying to start a career as a pop star.

---

- One of your coworkers has been bad-tempered recently.
- You got into an argument and said some unkind things to him.
- You found out that he has been dealing with serious health issues.

---

- Your parents have always dreamed that you would become a doctor.
- You are in medical school now, but you hate it.
- You want to quit, but don't know what to say to your parents.

---

- You are attending university in the United States.
- Your parents gave you enough money for the entire year.
- You wasted all of the money on a gambling trip in Las Vegas.

---

- You've been working for the last five years.
- You go out several times a week with friends.
- You haven't managed to save any money, and now you want to buy a house.

---

- You are in love with an incredible man/woman who you see every day on the bus.
- You've never talked to this person, so he/she doesn't even know who you are.

# C. Choices and Consequences

**PART 1** ● For each situation below, discuss which choice you would make and why. Use the boxes to keep track of your answers.

> **Example:**
> *I would keep the money because I'm not responsible for the waiter's mistakes.*

**1** At a restaurant, your waiter does not charge you for part of your meal.

**Would you**
a. let the waiter know about the mistake and give him the money back? ☐
b. keep the money? ☐

**2** You come across a young girl looking at a beautiful dress in a store window. You have a coupon for one free outfit.

**Would you**
a. give the girl your coupon so she can get the dress? ☐
b. get yourself a very stylish outfit? ☐

**3** You get to the bus stop a few seconds too late. The bus driver looks at you and smiles as he drives away.

**Would you**
a. wait patiently for the next bus? ☐
b. run after the bus, yelling and making rude gestures? ☐

**4** You arrive at your favorite restaurant for lunch. A very hungry-looking dog is sitting by the door looking at you. You only have a little money.

**Would you**
a. feed the dog? ☐
b. feed yourself? ☐

**5** You worked very late last night and got very little sleep. You're absolutely exhausted. You know your boss is out of the office today.

**Would you**
a. sleep in and be late to work, but well rested? ☐
b. force yourself to go to work on time? ☐

**6** You have to buy a new phone. You've put yourself on a budget so you can go on vacation.

**Would you**
a. buy the cheap phone that can only make phone calls and text for $15 a month? ☐
b. buy the expensive phone with lots of games and apps for $100 a month? ☐

## PART 2

> Look at the **consequences** of the decisions you made in Part 1.
> After you find out the consequences, discuss whether you regret your decision or not.
> If so, what could you have done differently?

> **Example:**
> I would keep the money because I'm not responsible for the waiter's mistakes.
> **A:** *The waiter lost his job. Do you regret your decision?*
> **B:** *That's really terrible. I guess I could've been honest and given back the money.*
> **C:** *I wouldn't regret it. He should've been more careful. It's his job.*

**1** ▶ a. The waiter thanks you for your honesty and gives you a coupon for a free meal.
b. Later that night, the waiter's boss accuses him of stealing. He is fired.

**2** ▶ a. The girl thanks you for the coupon. She goes inside and buys her boyfriend a jacket.
b. You wear your stylish outfit out to dinner. You spill wine on it. The outfit is ruined.

**3** ▶ a. It starts to rain while you wait for the next bus, and you don't have an umbrella.
b. You trip in the street from running. Everyone laughs at you as the bus drives away.

**4** ▶ a. The dog is so happy about the food that he starts following you everywhere.
b. You see the dog outside the restaurant for a few days. After a week, the dog disappears.

**5** ▶ a. Your boss came to work today! He yells at you for being two hours late.
b. You make your afternoon presentation but make lots of mistakes because you're so tired.

**6** ▶ a. You feel you're missing out on a bit of your social life, but you manage to save enough to go on vacation for a month.
b. When you go to buy travel tickets, you realize you don't have enough money. Instead of traveling overseas, you have to spend your vacation at home.

**consequence** *(n.):* result

# Discussion Questions

1. If you could go back in time and change one thing about your life, what would it be?
    ▶ Why do you think changing this thing would make a big difference to your life?

2. What are three things about your present situation that you would like to change?

3. Which bad habits do you have, and how have you tried to change them?

4. Who is someone you admire for having made positive changes in his/her life?

5. Can you **look back on** a moment in your life when you said something you probably shouldn't have said?
    ▶ When was it?
    ▶ Why did you say it?

6. Do you feel like you should have taken high school or university more seriously or less seriously? Why?

7. Is **hindsight** truly 20/20?
    ▶ Do you tend to **chew over** events that you cannot change, or do you have **no regrets**?

**UNIT 6 REVIEW**

**How well can you use:**
- ☐ Making guesses about the past (speculation)?
- ☐ Expressing regret?

What do you need to study more?

---

**chew over** *(phrasal verb):* to continue thinking about something after it is over
**hindsight** *(n.):* the understanding gained after an incident has occurred
**look back on (something)** *(phrasal verb):* to think about the past

# Activity: The Pie of Regret

Think of an answer for each of the following things…..

1 Something you should have remembered but forgot _____

2 Something you shouldn't have eaten _____

3 Something you shouldn't have bought _____

4 A day you should have stayed in bed _____

5 A place you shouldn't have gone _____

- Vague and precise language
- Giving reasons with because and since

- Now, imagine that the pie below is the total amount of your regret.
- Divide the pie into pieces with an approximate percentage for each of the above things.
- Then discuss what you regret more and why.

**Example:**

**A:** *What is something you shouldn't have eaten?*

**B:** *I shouldn't have eaten an entire pizza by myself when I was in university because it made me really sick.*

**A:** *Is that your biggest slice of regret?*

**B:** *No. It's only around twenty percent. I regret buying these shoes at full price a lot more.*

Regret!
**Regret 20%**

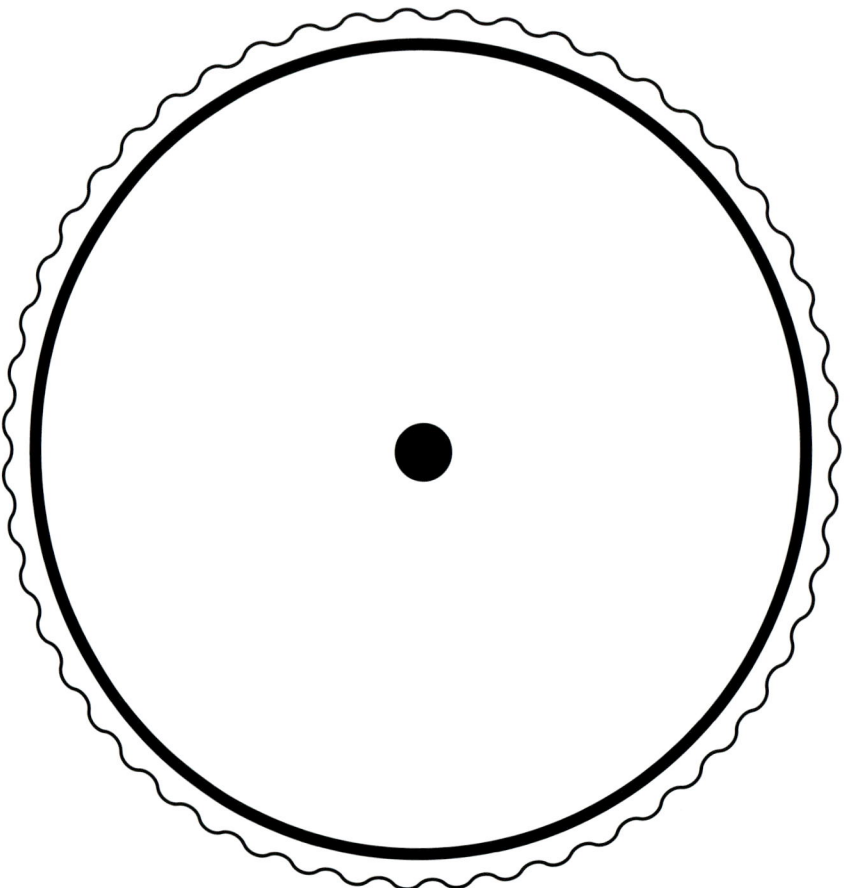

# Segue

# Where in the World is Mr. Squiggles?

### May 10th
Buenos dias. I live in Barcelona, Spain. One day a cat came floating up to the beach on a door! He seemed quite hungry, so I took him to a café where we ate tapas. We met a photographer who said he wanted to take his picture and disappeared after that. He could have gone away with the photographer.

### May 25th
Ahh yes. Good old Mr. Squiggles! I met him in a bar in Spain. On a photo shoot in Kenya we were surprised by a big lion in a tree. I thought I was done for, but Mr. Squiggles chased the lion off! I lost him after that. I heard a rumor he might have been on plane bound for Asia.

### May 29th
Sawatdee. I'm an elephant veterinarian. I met this Mr. Squiggles in Thailand, where he helped us care for sick elephants. I'm not sure where he is, though. He seemed to be very friendly with a tourist who was visiting. He must have left with her.

### June 10th
G'day! I met old Squiggles while on holiday. He came back to Australia with me. I told my brother about his ability to communicate with elephants and he decided to take him to Antarctica where he is doing research on penguins.

### June 19th
Hola. I am a scientist from Argentina. I met this cat on the Antarctic ice where he was doing an amazing penguin mating dance! I decided to introduce him to my cousin, who is a dancer in Brazil.

### June 25th
Tudo bon. I danced Samba with the Squiggles. He was the most talented dancing cat I have ever worked with. I took him with me on a tour of the United States, but he disappeared. I think he might have been kidnapped!

### June 30th
Howdy! We were on vacation in Hollywood when we saw this cat. My friend Darla told me he was an internet celebrity. So we grabbed him to get a photo in front of the Hollywood sign. He ran off though! He must have been scared.

## A. Discussion
1. Would you like to travel to any of the places mentioned on the blog?
   - If you could travel around the world for two months where would you go?
2. How do you think Mr. Squiggles might have traveled from one location to the next?

## B. Writing
Write a short blog posting like the ones above saying you have seen Mr. Squiggles in your country and guess what you think might have happened to him.

# 07
# Make Yourself at Home
## Culture and Nation Building

**Objectives:**
/ Adding to imperatives
/ Listen to a story about a trip

## WARM UP

What are some of the customs in your country for…

> …dining?
> …talking to an authority figure? (parent/boss/teacher)
> …greeting a new acquaintance?
> …dating?

### IDIOMS

- **Culture shock**
- **Go with the flow**

    When I first saw people kissing each other for a greeting, I felt a little bit of *culture shock*. But I figured I should *go with the flow*.

### PHRASAL VERBS

- **Blend in**
- **Stick out**

    It was very hard for me to *blend in* when I went to study abroad. I was the only person with my skin color, and I really *stuck out*.

### COLLOCATIONS

- **Cultural norms**
- **Table manners**

    Every country has its own *cultural norms* that they follow. For example, in some countries it is polite *table manners* to belch after eating.

### TONGUE TWISTER

Betty Botter bought a bit of butter,
but the butter Betty bought was bitter;
so Betty bought a bit of better butter to make
the bitter butter better.

# LESSON 1

## A. Don't Even Think About It

**Language Point : Dos and Don'ts**

The **imperative form** is often used to give instructions, commands, and directions.

It is also used to give strong definite advice about behavior and expectations.
▸ When you eat at your Grandmother's house, **don't mention** the terrible burning smell.

It is good to add a reason to an imperative so the listener knows why they need to follow the instructions.
▸ Eat all your food **because** it's important to respect your elders.
Bring a gift **so that** you don't make a bad impression.

**PART 1**
What are some things you do or don't do when…

1. Talking to your parents?
2. Sitting in class?
3. Eating at a restaurant?
4. Riding the subway?
5. Attending a funeral?
6. Going on a first date?
7. Visiting someone's home?
8. Going to a movie?

# PART 2

Match the Dos and Don'ts with the reasons why they are important. Ask a follow up question.

**Example:**
**A:** *What should I be careful about when visiting Nepal?*
**B:** *When visiting Nepal, don't eat food off the same plate as others because it's considered unclean.*
**A:** *Really? Do you agree with that? Have you ever visited Nepal?*

**1**

**A:** What should I be careful about when visiting Greece?
**B:** When visiting Greece, don't eat your dessert too quickly because...

**3**

**A:** What should I be careful about when visiting China?
**B:** When visiting China, don't give someone a watch for a present because.....

**2**

**A:** What should I be careful about when visiting France?
**B:** When visiting France, don't bring wine to someone's house for dinner because...

**4**

**A:** What should I be careful about when visiting Thailand?
**B:** When visiting Thailand, don't touch anyone with your foot because...

A. ripping it with your teeth looks low class.

B. it looks like you're counting the time until they die.

C. eating everything makes you look like a pig.

D. your host will think you want to leave.

E. it is considered the dirtiest part of the body.

F. you are telling the hosts they have poor taste.

**5**

**A:** What should I be careful about when visiting Italy?
**B:** When visiting Italy, use your hands to break bread because...

**6**

**A:** What should I be careful about when visiting Brazil?
**B:** When visiting Brazil, leave a little food on your plate because...

# B. Life Tips from Grandpa

## Language Point : Adding Adverbs to the Imperative Form

**Adverbs** can be used to say **how or how often** something needs to be done.
> Pack your souvenirs **carefully** because you don't want them to break in your luggage. **Never** leave your bag unattended.

### Pre-listening

Where is an interesting place you have traveled?
> What are some of the dos and don'ts of traveling in that place?

### Listening  TRACK 14-15

While listening complete the chart with the advice Grandpa gives Lisa.

| | |
|---|---|
| Travel _____ | cautiously |
| Hold onto your _____ | tightly. |
| Definitely _____ | go on a _____ |
| | take the subway. |
| Carefully _____ | _____ the map because the subway is _____ |
| Absolutely _____ | |
| | go out with friends. |
| Never _____ | _____ on the streets alone and _____ to strangers. |

### Post-listening

Travel advice: Match an adverb to an imperative and the reason why.

| Adverbs | Dos and don'ts | Reasons |
|---|---|---|
| Always | Go with the flow | Because you don't want to carry heavy luggage everywhere. |
| Never | Know what is not allowed | So that you can be flexible in your schedule. |
| Carefully | Overplan | Because customs and attitude can be different in other countries. |
| Definitely | Pack your suitcase | So that you don't get into an embarrassing situation. |

1. What advice would you give to someone going overseas by themselves for the first time?
2. Would you recommend anything to do or not do when visiting Paris?

**go with the flow** *(idiom)*: to do what other people are doing

# C. Mystery Chef

## Language Point : Imperatives in Sequence

**Time words** are used to say **when** or in what order something should be done.

▸ *First, heat a pan. Then, carefully break an egg so that you don't get egg shell in the pan.*

### Do You Remember?

- At the beginning of instructions, use expressions like: **First..., To begin..., First of all...**
- To sequence instructions, use expressions like: **Then..., Next..., After that..., Second...**
- At the end of instructions, use expressions like: **Finally..., To finish..., Lastly...**

**PART 1** •

Unscramble the steps of some recipes that are common in English-speaking countries. Describe the recipe to your partner using time words. After describing the recipe, check the next page to see if your description was correct!

### DENVER OMELET

*Ingredients:* oil, eggs, ham, onion, bell pepper, cheese

Procedure:

___ Fry onion, bell pepper, and ham in a pan with oil.

___ Pour the fried onion, pepper and ham mixture on top of the cooked eggs.

___ Cook the eggs.

___ **Whisk** the eggs.

___ Top with cheese.

___ Pour the egg mixture onto the pan.

___ Crack eggs into a bowl.

### BREAD PUDDING

*Ingredients:* bread, milk, eggs, butter, dried fruit, sugar, spices

Procedure:

___ Pour the mixed ingredients into a pan.

___ Wait for a few minutes.

___ Cut the bread into pieces.

___ Mix the cut bread with milk.

___ Bake the mixture.

___ Enjoy!

___ Mix the bread and milk with eggs, butter, dried fruit, sugar, and spices.

**whisk** *(v.)*: to stir lightly

## PART 2

Now choose a recipe that you like or that is popular in your country. Explain the steps of the recipe to your partner. Use some of the recipe-related verbs to help you explain the procedure.

### Example: Mashed Potatoes

Ingredients: milk, potatoes, butter, salt, pepper

> *First*, wash and peel the potatoes. **Carefully** peel the potatoes **because** you don't want pieces of peel in the mashed potatoes.
> *Second*, boil the potatoes until they are soft.
> *Next*, mash the potatoes **gently so that** they have a good texture.
> *After that*, add salt, pepper, butter, and milk to the potatoes. **Slowly** add the salt **so that** the potatoes are not too salty.
> *Finally*, stir the ingredients together and enjoy!

 Cut

Stir

Mash

 Top

 Recipe

Fry

 Flip

 Boil

 Bake

 Peel

### Denver Omelet

**Ingredients:** oil, eggs, ham, onion, bell pepper, cheese

**Procedure**
(time words may vary):

1. First, fry onion, bell pepper and ham in a pan with oil and set aside for later.
2. After that, crack eggs into a bowl.
3. Then, whisk the eggs.
4. Next, pour the egg mixture into a pan.
5. After that, cook the eggs.
6. Finally, pour the fried onion, pepper and ham mixture on top of the cooked egg.
7. To finish, top with cheese.

### Bread Pudding

**Ingredients:** bread, milk, eggs, butter, dried fruit, sugar, spices

**Procedure**
(time words may vary):

1. First, cut the bread into pieces.
2. Second, mix the cut bread with milk.
3. Then, wait for a few minutes.
4. After that, mix the bread and milk with eggs, butter, dried fruit, sugar, and spices.
5. Next, pour the mixed ingredients into a pan.
6. Then, bake the mixture.
7. Finally, enjoy!

 Shred

 Pour

 Mix

# Discussion Questions

1. What were some of the dos and don'ts that you were taught as a child? For example, **table manners**, talking to strangers, etc.
   - Are they the same dos and don'ts that you (will) teach your own children?

2. What are some **cultural norms** that people visiting your country might have a hard time understanding?

3. What are the dos and don'ts of **tipping** in your culture?
   - How do these dos and don'ts differ from those of other countries?

4. What kinds of warning signs do you see while you are driving or walking on the street?
   - What do the signs tell you to do or not do?

5. What are some dos and don'ts for using a cell phone?
   - Do you think cell phone culture is making people ruder? Why?

6. What are some workplace dos and don'ts?
   - How about classroom dos and don'ts?

7. Do you find instruction manuals for devices like MP3 players, digital cameras, and computers to be useful?
   - Do you often read instruction manuals?

**cultural norm** *(idiom)*: behavior that is expected within a society
**table manners** *(collocation)*: the way that a person acts while dining at a table
**tip** *(v.)*: to give money in exchange for service

# LESSON 2

## >> WARM UP

You have been invited to a very formal state dinner at the United Nations. See if you can make a guess about what all the different items in the formal dinner setting are used for.

**Objectives:**
/ Nation Building

# A. These Are My People

**PART 1** • You have been chosen as the next Great Leaders of one of the following societies. Choose one or make your own.

| | | | | | |
|---|---|---|---|---|---|
| **Nation** |  Free Cake |  Squigglosia |  Humberg |  Costa Lotsa |  KipiKipi |
| **Motto** | "Let Us Eat Cake!" | "Pet Me, Feed Me!" | "Tradition!" | "Show Me the Money!" | "KIPI KIPI!" |
| **Leader Type** | President | Lord | King or Queen | CEO | Prime Minister |
| **Population** | 200,000 | 650,000 | 8,100,000 | 3,300,000 | 70,000 |
| **Biggest Export** |  Food |  Natural Resources |  Labor |  Technology |  Entertainment |
| **Land Type** |  Plains |  Forests and Series of Islands |  Mountains and Deserts |  Snowy Plains and Mountains |  Jungles |
| **Biggest Problem** | Obesity | Large divide between rich and poor | Overpopulation | Pollution | Natural Disasters |

## Your Nation

| | |
|---|---|
| **Motto** | |
| **Leader Type** | |
| **Population** | |
| **Biggest Export** | |
| **Land Type** | |
| **Biggest Problem** | |

## PART 2

As leaders of your new nations, you must decide on some of the customs of your people. You have been asked to pass a series of laws. With your partner(s), decide which of the three options you will choose for your nation.

| Greetings | Shake hands | Bow | Kiss and hug |
|---|---|---|---|
| Fashion | All citizens wear a uniform that displays their social status. | People are free to wear any clothing they desire. | Everyone wears the exact same outfit to avoid **discrimination.** |
| Food | All food is made as a tasteless paste with all necessary nutrients. | Eating is a social experience. Tasty food that potentially leads to obesity and other health problems is common. | Everyone is required to grow their own food. |
| Education | Very strict educational system. Students are required to go to school for at least 15 years. | Educational system in which students are able to learn for themselves. | Children do not attend school; instead they learn by working as interns from a young age. |
| Work | Jobs are assigned by the government. | There is freedom to do any job, but the society is highly competitive. | Every year, people are given a new job. |
| Money | There is no money. The government gives out necessities. | There is a free market system. | There is a **barter** system where all items are traded for items or services of equal value. |
| Entertain-ment | Every individual should be a part of the nation's entertainment industry for at least 15 minutes of their life. | Entertainment is made only with government approval so nothing offensive is presented. | There is no entertainment as it corrupts those who use it. |
| Social structure | Challenge authority to strengthen society. | Obey authority to strengthen society. | Most major decisions are made by a supercomputer. |

**discrimination** *(n.)*: unfair treatment of a person or group
**barter** *(v.)*: to exchange services or goods without using money

# B. Cultural Perspective

**Argue for or against each opinion** – the symbol of your nation determines which side of the argument you must take.

## FOR                                          AGAINST

 Internet and television should be censored by the government.

 Children should be raised by the entire community so everyone is responsible.

 Food and dietary concerns should be strictly dictated by the government to prevent health problems or obesity.

 The old and sick should be sent away in order to strengthen society.

 Every man and woman should serve in the military before being allowed to use any service paid for by tax dollars.

 Very attractive people should be forced to get ugly tattoos. Unattractive people should be forced to get makeovers.

**censor** *(v.)*: to restrict in order to prevent threats to security/authority

# C. Model Five Nations

## The Five Nations

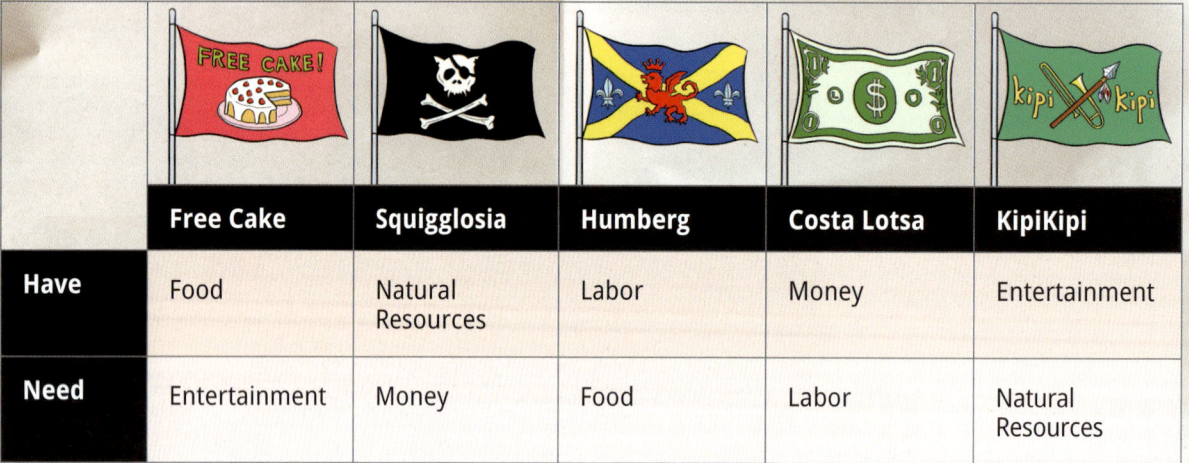

| | Free Cake | Squigglosia | Humberg | Costa Lotsa | KipiKipi |
|---|---|---|---|---|---|
| **Have** | Food | Natural Resources | Labor | Money | Entertainment |
| **Need** | Entertainment | Money | Food | Labor | Natural Resources |

Now that you've discussed the dos and don'ts for your society (as well as their world view based on Activity B) you must resolve the following issues in cooperation with the other societies. For each situation ask the following questions:

- What should we do?
- What could we have done to avoid the problem?
- How can your country help?

**Example:**
Many people from Humberg are trying to immigrate to its neighbor Squigglosia

A: *They could send the people to Costa Lotsa in exchange for technology.*

B: *Humberg should have trained them as singers. Then they could trade with Free Cake for food.*

1 There was a drought in Free Cake. Because of this, all nations are suffering a food shortage.

2 There is a conflict between KipiKipi and Squigglosia. Squigglosia refuses to give needed resources to KipiKipi because the news media of KipiKipi said some very bad things about the government of Squigglosia.

3 There was an earthquake in Humberg. Thousands are in need of aid. Based on your nation's exports, what specific aid can you send to help?
   ▶ If you are Humberg, what do you need? How can you help your people?

4 There will be an international sports competition in which all nations will compete. Everyone wants to hold the event.

5 A group of hackers in Costa Lotsa revealed that the Great Leaders of each nation are making a huge amount of money. People have started protesting all over the world because they think it is unfair.

6 Scientists from every nation are seeing an increase in global warming.

 **Bonus** Work together to discuss solutions to each nation's biggest problems mentioned in Activity A.

# Discussion Questions

**1** What are some of the things that define your culture?
- ▶ What do people think about when they think about your country?

**2** What are some of the common forms of greeting in your country?
- ▶ How would you greet someone older than you?
- ▶ How would you greet someone younger than you?

**3** What countries do you feel like you can visit and **blend in** to the population?
- ▶ What countries have you visited where you felt like you really **stuck out**?

**4** What are some of the most popular foods in your country? Which of these foods do you like and dislike?
- ▶ What are some of your favorite foods from other countries?

**5** If you had to choose one place to live for the rest of your life, where would you choose to live?
- ▶ Why would you choose that place?

**6** Air travel has made it possible for people to go around the world in less than a day.
- ▶ What are some of the pros and cons of air travel?

**7** Have you ever experienced **culture shock** when traveling in your own country or overseas?
- ▶ What happened?

**8** Do you think that when you are visiting another country you should go with the flow or keep your own customs?

**UNIT 7 REVIEW**

**How well can you use:**
- ☐ Expressing dos and don'ts?
- ☐ Using adverbs, reasons, and time with imperatives?

What do you need to study more?

---

**blend in** *(phrasal verb):* to be difficult to distinguish from the surroundings
**culture shock** *(n.):* surprise felt from exposure to a new culture
**stick out** *(phrasal verb):* to be easy to distinguish from the surroundings

# Activity: Dinner Party Dilemma

**PART 1** ● In your group, discuss your food preferences using the list below for guidance. Be sure to ask each group member if there are any foods they hate.

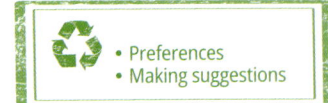
- Preferences
- Making suggestions

- Chocolate or vanilla
- Rice or bread
- Cheese or tofu
- Broccoli or corn
- Apples or pears
- Beef or seafood
- Grapes or cherries
- Coffee or tea
- Eggs or beans
- Potatoes or noodles
- Lettuce or tomatoes
- Other preferences...?

**Example:**
**A:** *Do you prefer broccoli or corn?*
**B:** *I definitely prefer broccoli. Actually, I hate corn!*
**A:** *Really? I love corn.*

**PART 2** ● Based on your preferences, plan a meal that everyone in the group will eat. The meal must include a soup, a main dish, a drink, and a dessert.

**Example:**
**A:** *We shouldn't have corn soup since you don't like corn. What kind of soup should we have?*
**B:** *I suggest that we have chicken soup.*

Dessert

Drink

Main Dish

Soup

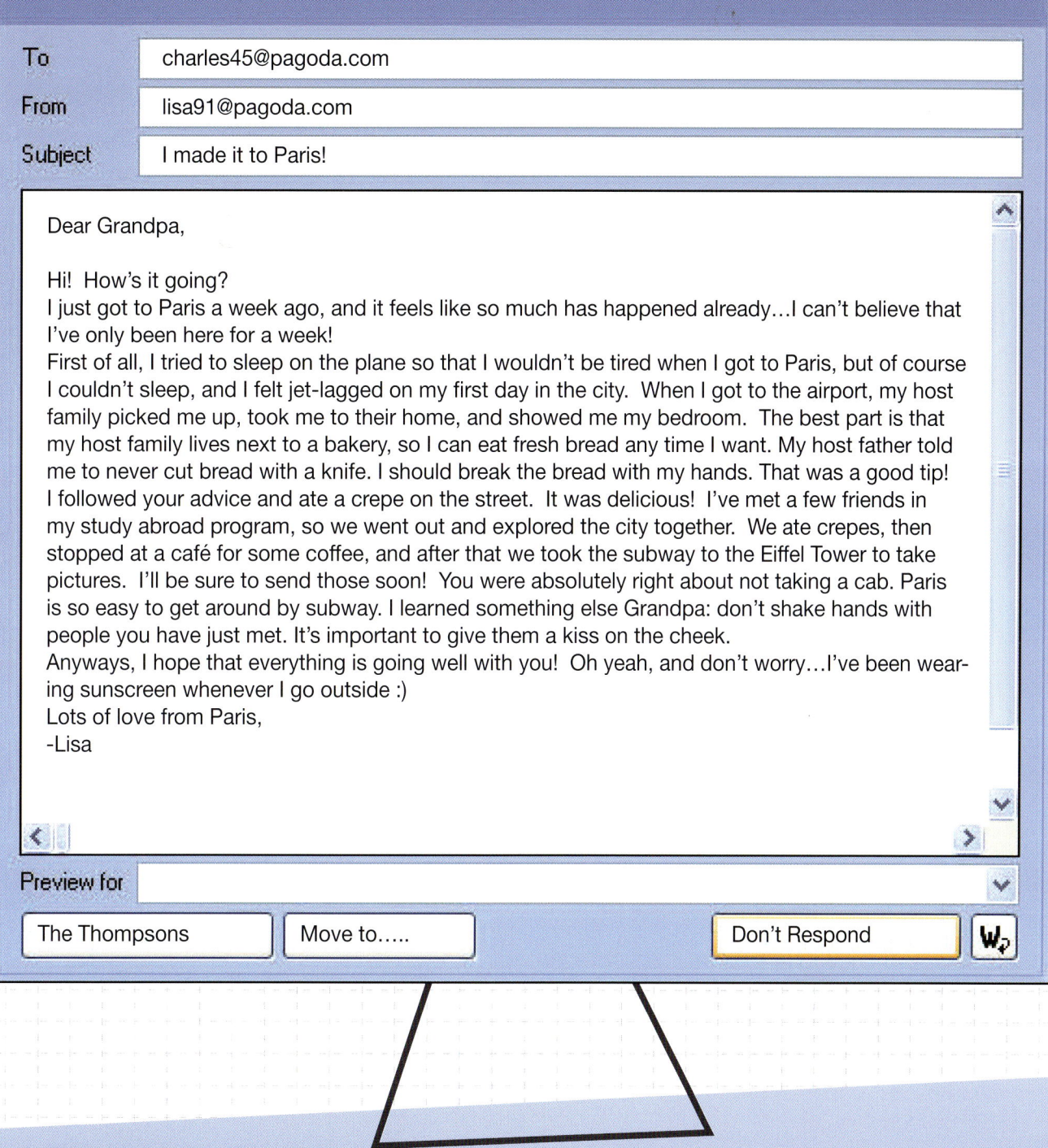

## A. Discussion
1. Do you think Lisa's experience in Paris sounds like fun so far? Why or why not?
2. If you had the opportunity to study abroad anywhere in the world, where would you want to go? Why?

## B. Writing
1. Write an email to your teacher describing some important things he or she should do in your country.
2. Write an email to your teacher describing some cultural dos and don'ts you have experienced while traveling abroad.

## WARM UP

**Tell me about……..**

- Your home.
- Your neighborhood.
- Who you live with.
- Your landlord.
- The last time you moved.
- The last party you went to.

## IDIOMS

- **Crash**
  I'm exhausted. I think I'll go home and *crash*.
- **In the sticks**
  Her house is really nice, but it is way out *in the sticks*.

## COLLOCATIONS

- **Next-door neighbor**
  My *next-door neighbor* keeps me up all night with his T.V.
- **At home**
  I prefer spending time *at home* instead of going out.

## PHRASAL VERBS

- **Move in/out**
  We rented the apartment and we can *move in* next week.
- **Put up**
  My brother just *moved out* of his place and I said I would *put him up* for a few days.

## TONGUE TWISTER

You know New York.
You need New York.
You know you need unique New York.

Unit 8  The Grass is Always Greener  |  135

# LESSON 1

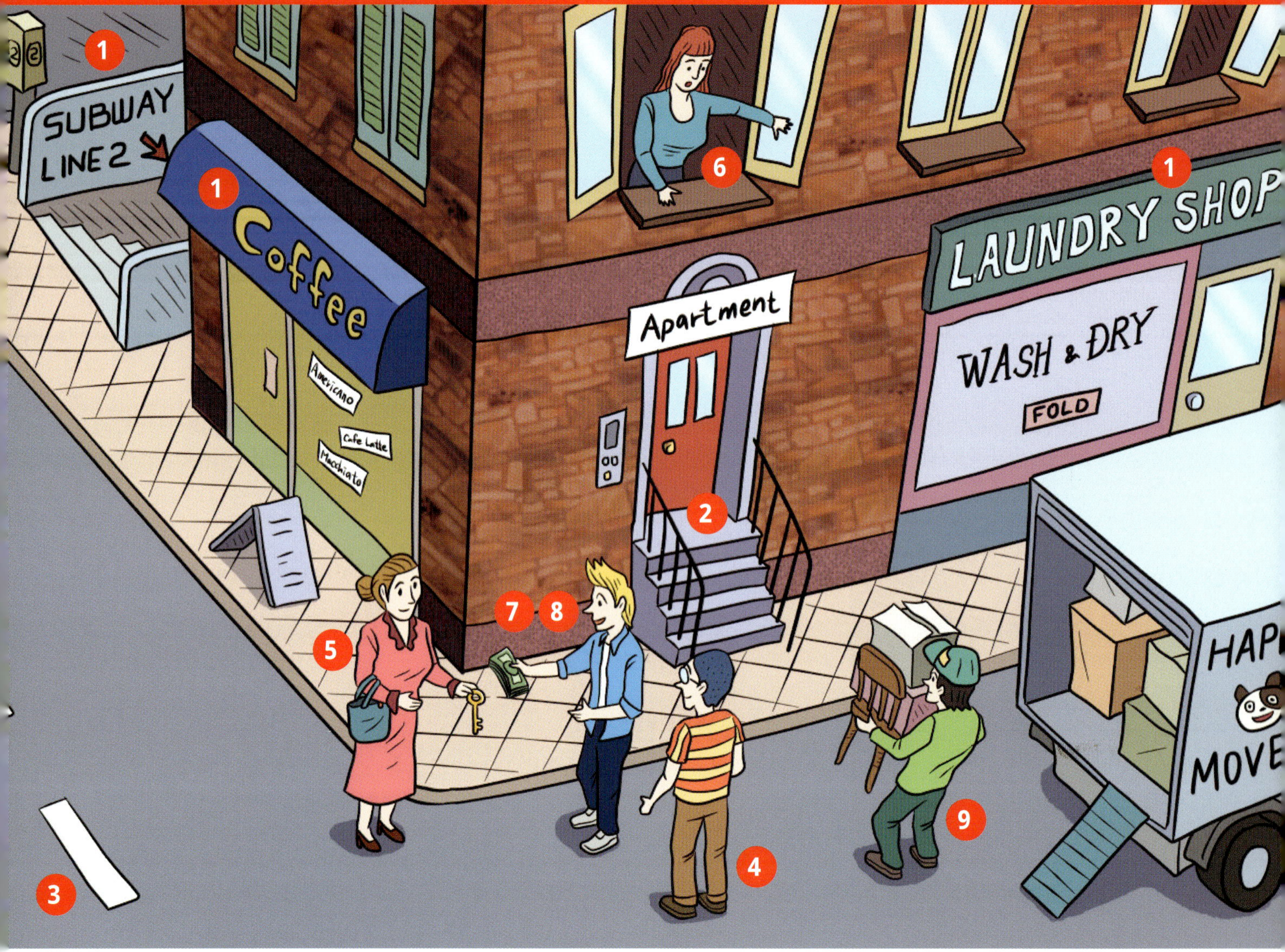

## A. Whose House? Jack's House.

**Places**
Amenities : 1
Apartment/Flat : 2
Neighborhood : 3

**People**
Roommate : 4
Landlord : 5
Neighbors : 6

**Things**
Rent : 7
Deposit : 8
Moving : 9

**deposit** *(n.)*: a one-time returnable sum given for rental of property
**rent** *(n.)*: a regular payment for housing

Discuss your current living situation. Ask questions regarding the different aspects of where you live. Then, ask a follow up question about what your ideal situation would be for each topic.

**1** The amenities near your house
- Currently...
- Ideally.....

**2** Your home
- Currently....
- Ideally....

**3** Who you live with
- Currently....
- Ideally....

**4** Your neighbors
- Currently....
- Ideally....

**5** Your **cost of living**
- Currently...
- Ideally...

**6** Your furniture
- Currently...
- Ideally....

**Example:**
How many times you have moved

**A:** *How many times have you moved in your life?*

**B:** *Let's see......About thirty.*

**C:** *Thirty! Why so many?*

**A:** *My dad was in the military. Ideally, I wish I had moved only three or four times.*

**cost of living** *(n.)*: average cost for basic necessities such as food and housing

Unit 8 The Grass is Always Greener | 137

# B. Odd Couple

## Pre-listening

1. What issues do you have to deal with when living with another person?
2. Which of the following people would you like to have as your roommate? Why?

### Nell

- Cleans every day
- Works all day, listens to music all night
- Has a very large dog
- Has friends over once or twice a month
- Borrows things without asking.

### Herman

- Cleans once a week
- Always home
- Has several cats, a bird, and a few fish
- Has no friends

### Roxy

- Cleans whenever she sees something dirty
- Only around on weekends
- Allergic to pets
- Has a boyfriend who stays with her some weekends

### Jack

- Cleans when asked
- In and out of the house frequently
- Wants a pet but doesn't want to take care of a pet
- Friends often come over to watch movies and play video games

## Listening  TRACK 16-17

Jack has to decide between two possible roommates. Look at the picture to see the lifestyles of Antoine and George. What can you guess about each of their personalities based on their apartment? Listen to the dialogue and guess which roommate Jack would choose based on his own personality.

## Post-listening

Compare preferences with your partner to see if you would make good roommates.

toiletries (n.): items used for hygiene

# C. Pagoda 21 Realty

**PART 1** ● You and your partner are roommates. Look at the housing ads below, and discuss your opinion of each place. After discussing each of the possibilities, choose one place as your new home.

### Apartment for rent: 1

- 2 bedroom, 1 bath
- Pets allowed
- Includes **utilities**
- Indoor pool and sauna
- Banquet room
- Air conditioning
- Close to all amenities
- Newly painted
- $1,000/mnth (1/2 mnth rent damage deposit)

**Island Management, 604-555-6933**

### Townhouse for rent: 2

- 2 bedroom, 2 bath
- Close to parks and downtown
- Fitness center and steam room
- Only small pets allowed
- Newly renovated
- Includes cable
- 2 parking spaces
- 1 year lease
- References required
- $1,400/mnth (1 month rent damage deposit)

**E-mail: rick@realestate.com**

### House for rent: 5

- 2 bedroom, 1 bath
- Beautiful garden, easy to maintain
- Plenty of parking in garage
- Storage
- Large windows with great view of valley
- Hot tub and outdoor pool
- No pets
- Hardwood floors
- $1,500/mnth (1/2 month rent damage deposit)

**Contact Gunter Realty, 504-555-7116**

### Penthouse apartment for rent: 6

- 4 bedroom, 4 bath
- 2 floors
- 2 balconies
- Indoor pool and sauna
- Private elevator
- Security system
- Close to the lake and golf course
- Spa facilities
- $5,500/mnth (1 month rent damage deposit)

**Visit: www.luxuryrentals.com**

**Example:**

**A:** *Hmm...I like number four, the condo, because it has a gym! Plus, if we share the rent then we won't have to pay too much each month.*

**B:** *Number four looks good, but no pets are allowed. What will I do with my pet kitten?*

### Basement suite for rent  3

- 2 bedroom, 1 bathroom
- Private entrance
- Close to schools, universities, and parks
- Close to public transportation
- Walk-in closets and large kitchen
- Includes utilities
- Pets allowed (with references)
- Fully-furnished
- References required
- $850/mnth (1/2 month rent damage deposit)

**Call: Mrs. Hinkle, 504-555-7116**

### Condo for rent:  4

- 3 bedroom, 2 bath
- Nice area
- Gym and mini golf green
- No pets allowed
- No smoking
- 20 min from shops and bus stop
- Heat and hot water included
- Free internet
- One parking space
- $1,100/mnth (1 month rent damage deposit)

**E-mail: townsend@rentalproperty.com**

PAGODA 21 REALTY

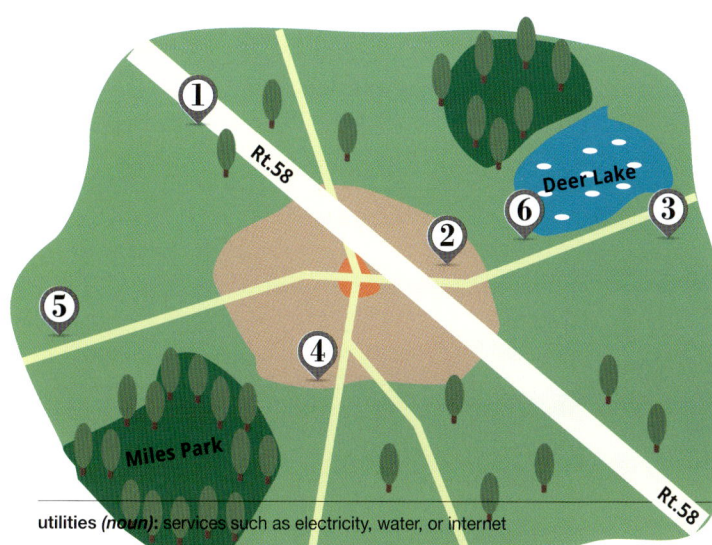

**Housing locations are listed on this map.**

**Major highway and subway routes, local parks, and Deer Lake are also listed.**

**utilities** *(noun)*: services such as electricity, water, or internet

Unit 8 The Grass is Always Greener

## PART 2

You've chosen your dream home! However, now that you've finally moved in, you're having some problems. Discuss with your partner/roommate how you could resolve the issues below.

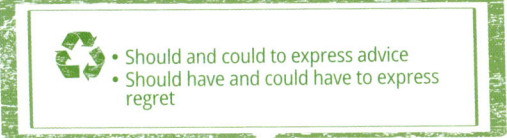
- Should and could to express advice
- Should have and could have to express regret

**Example:** The price of heating has gone up significantly this winter.
**A:** We should have rented the basement suite. Heating wouldn't have been so expensive.
**B:** We should chop down a tree in the front yard and burn wood in the fireplace to keep warm.
**C:** We could get a new roommate to help out with the cost.

1. Due to some plumbing problems, all of the water in your home must be turned off for a week.

2. The city has discontinued the bus line near your apartment, and now it takes 20 minutes to walk to the nearest public transportation.

3. Your neighbor has loud parties almost every night, and they disrupt your sleep.

4. There is a large water leak in the ceiling.

5. Your home is infested with cockroaches.

6. A friend of yours asked if she could stay for a while. You said okay, but it has been several weeks now and she is not paying any rent.

# Discussion Questions

1. Do you like moving? Why or why not?
   - How long does it take you to fully **move in** to a new house?

2. If you could choose to live in any kind of place, which kind would you choose?

3. What kind of person would you consider an ideal **next-door neighbor**?
   - How about the worst next-door neighbor? Why?

4. How would our lives be different if the modern technology that helps make our home lives easier did not exist?
   - What modern **conveniences** could you not live without?

5. What are the advantages and disadvantages of where you live?
   - If you could make changes to the area where you live, what would they be? Why?

6. Are you the type of person who likes to live alone or with other people?
   - What are the advantages of living by yourself?
   - What are the advantages of living with others?
   - Would you ever **put a friend up** at your home for a few days?

7. What time do you usually **crash**?
   - Do you spend more time outside the house or do you prefer staying at home?

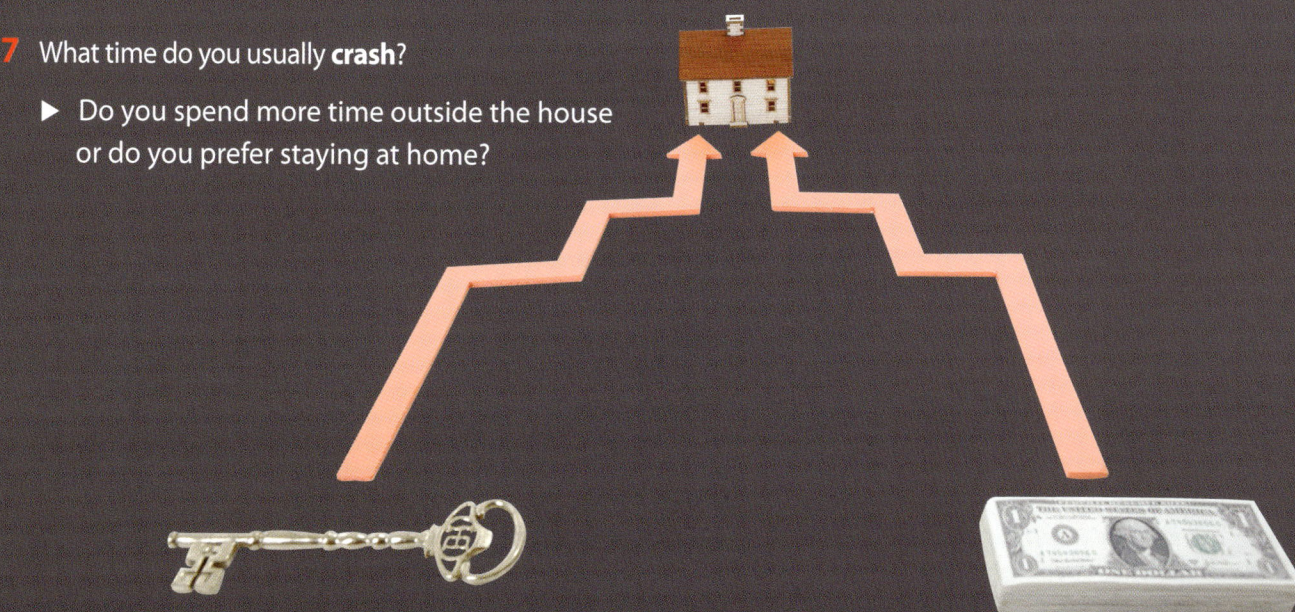

**convenience** *(n.)*: things that make life easier
**crash** *(idiom)*: to sleep
**move in** *(phrasal verb)*: occupy a house
**next door neighbor** *(n.)*: someone who lives in the home next to one's own home
**put up** *(phrasal verb)*: to allow a person to stay at one's home

# LESSON 2

>> WARM UP

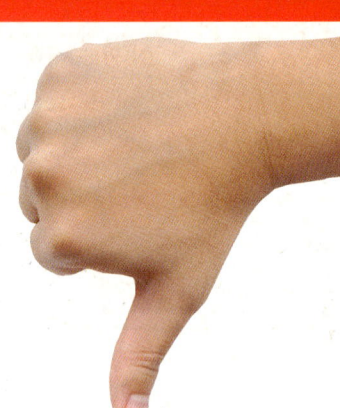

Brainstorm: What are the pros and cons of…

## Pros                                    ## Cons

…having a roommate?

…losing your cell phone?

…living in an apartment?

…being locked out of your house?

…eating out?

…losing your luggage on vacation?

# A. Cousin Squaggles

What are some of the **upsides** and **downsides** of life in urban and rural areas? Consider the topics listed below.

> **Do You Remember? Complaining**
>
> - **Too much/many + noun** and **not enough + noun**
>   There are **too many mosquitoes** in my house.
>   There's always **too much traffic** in the city.
>
> - **Too + adjective** and **not + adjective + enough**
>   That apartment looks **too small**.
>   I'm **not wealthy enough** to buy a house.

Rural / Urban

- One of the downsides of living in a rural area is that there is **not enough public transportation**.
- One advantage of living in a rural area is that it's easy to have pets.

- One of the cons of living in a city is that schools are **too crowded**.
- One of the upsides of living in an urban area is lots of shopping!

**TOPICS:**

Pets

Traffic

Housing

Pollution

Shopping

Education

Arts and Entertainment

Parks and Outdoor Space

Transportation

**downside** *(n.)*: disadvantage
**upside** *(n.)*: advantage

# B. Silver Linings

## Language Point : Contrasting Negatives

When complaining, speakers often try to contrast negatives with positives. This is called finding the **silver lining**.

> ### Contrasting: turning a negative into a positive
> - **Even though** *Even though there's always too much traffic in the city, the transportation is better.*
> - **But** *That apartment looks too small, but it's really close to the subway.*

**PART 1** ● Look at the pictures below and describe what problems the pictures show. Then try to contrast the negative with a positive.

Earl Jr.

**Example:**
**A:** *Earl's boots and hat are way **too big** for him.*
**B:** *They might not be small enough, **but** he'll be able to wear them a long time.*
**C:** *Earl's mom's dress is **too short** for a mom.*
**A:** *Well, **even though** her dress isn't **long enough**, she and Earl can share accessories.*

Earl's Mom

January at Big Beach

Jack's apartment

Sue's Truck

Big Boy $12.00

August at Big Beach

Joan's apartment

Bob's Car

Rare Steak $22.00

## PART 2

Try to think of something you don't like about the following things, and then think of something positive about them.

> **Example: Countryside**
> **A:** *There are way **too many** insects in the country and **not enough** amenities.*
> **B:** *Well, **even though** there are too many insects, the air is really clean and there are fresh vegetables.*

1. Local transportation
2. The last place you traveled
3. The weather
4. The place where you work/ go to school
5. Your living situation
6. Housing in your area

# C. Susan's Catering Nightmare

Tonight there is a housewarming party for a very important client. You and your partners have been put in charge, but everything seems to be going wrong! You must work together to get through the party. Flip a coin to move squares (heads: one space, tails: two spaces). Take turns responding to the situation. Your partner(s) will take on the role of the person you are talking to.

**Example:** After someone ordered drinks, the waiter never came back!

**A:** *I am so sorry about the poor service. I will find a waiter to help you. This won't happen again!*

**B:** *We have been waiting for almost twenty minutes! I don't want a waiter, I want my drink!*

**A:** *I understand completely. I will personally go get your drink right now.*

**B:** *Thank you. That sounds great. And make sure there's plenty of ice!*

**START**

There are not enough spoons for the dinner guests! Apologize and find a solution.

You see a server cleaning a spoon with his shirt.

The balloons are blue. They were supposed to be red! Apologize and find the silver lining.

Bobo the Clown is willing to sell you balloons, but he wants way too much money for them. Complain to Bobo.

Your head chef was an hour late. Chew him out!

Your dishwasher wants to quit because she works too many hours. Help her find the silver lining.

The soup is cold. Apologize and find the silver lining.

You sample your soup. Lose a turn.

Your server is texting during work. Tell her to get back to work.

The neighbors are having a noisy party next door. Get them to turn down the music.

You forgot to include a vegetarian dish! Apologize to the vegetarian and find a solution.

You run to the market. Lose a turn.

A rival catering company shows up. Tell them to leave!

A woman's three young children are misbehaving during dinner. Ask her to control them.

A chef wrote the wrong name on the cake! Complain to the chef then apologize to the client.

You're exhausted! Complain about having too much work. Lose a turn.

You ate too much. Describe your feelings.

The main dish is delicious! Compliment your chef and move forward one space.

Your musician came to the event drunk! Complain and find a solution.

The raffle prize is missing and the winner has already been announced. Apologize and find a solution.

Someone left the cake out in the rain. Talk to the server responsible, apologize to the client and find a solution.

The brownie dessert is too delicious! There is not enough for everybody. Apologize to the guests and find a solution.

Your client doesn't want to pay full price. Explain why you should be paid. Get your money!

**FINISH**

# Discussion Questions

1 What are the advantages and disadvantages of renting a home rather than buying one?
   ▶ What are the advantages and disadvantages of buying a home?

2 Would you rather live in the sticks or in the middle of the city?
   ▶ What are the advantages and disadvantages to each?

3 When you have an important decision to make and have to choose between two options, what do you usually do?
   ▶ Do you make a list of pros and cons for each option or do you use another method?

4 Are you the kind of person who generally goes along with others' opinions or are you strongly opinionated?

5 What are the advantages and disadvantages of working hard?

6 Are there any advantages to eating **junk food**?
   ▶ Which types of junk food do you prefer?

7 Do you agree that every situation in life has pros and cons?
   ▶ Can you think of any situation that has only upsides or downsides?

## UNIT 8 REVIEW

**How well can you use:**
☐ Expressions about living situations?
☐ Complaining and Contrasting?
What do you need to study more?

**junk food** *(idiom)*: food that does not benefit a person's health

# Activity: Spin Doctor

- Pros and cons
- Expressing complaints using too/enough
- Expressing contrast using even though/but

### PART 1

The city of Silverson is holding elections for mayor. However, all of the candidates have some downsides. Imagine that you are a **spin doctor** for one of the candidates. Prepare a public relations campaign to share with the class that focuses on the silver lining of the candidate's downsides. Think about…

- Why the problems are actually good.
  **Example:** *Even though Bobby Smith's texting at meetings can be annoying, he's good at **multitasking**!*
- Specific examples of how the candidate's problems will help them to be a good mayor.
  **Example:** *Bobby Smith's multitasking skills will help him to manage the many demands of being mayor.*

### Candidate 1: Bobby Smith

**Pros:**
- Has been a politician for more than 10 years, so he has a lot of political experience.
- Started many businesses in the city, which created jobs for city residents.

**Cons:**
- Neighbors report that he frequently holds loud late-night parties at his house.
- Opened three factories that dumped pollution into the local river.
- Often eats potato chips and texts during important meetings.

### Candidate 2: Sally Sandal

**Pros:**
- Has an advanced degree (Ph.D.) in political science from a well-known university.
- Did a lot of volunteer work in college, so she is very popular in the local community.

**Cons:**
- Because of her busy schedule, Sally is rarely home and does not clean the apartment.
- Recently graduated from university and has no experience as a politician.
- Has strong ideas and does not compromise easily with others.

### Part 2
It's time for a television interview with the spin doctors!
- Your teacher will assign some students to be spin doctors and other students to be television interviewers.
- The interviewer group will prepare tough questions about the candidates' flaws.
- The spin doctors will prepare to talk about the silver lining of their candidate.
- The interviewers will interview each spin doctor committee about their candidate.

**multitask** *(v.)*: to do a variety of activities at the same time
**spin doctor** *(n.)*: a person who is able to present all information in a positive way

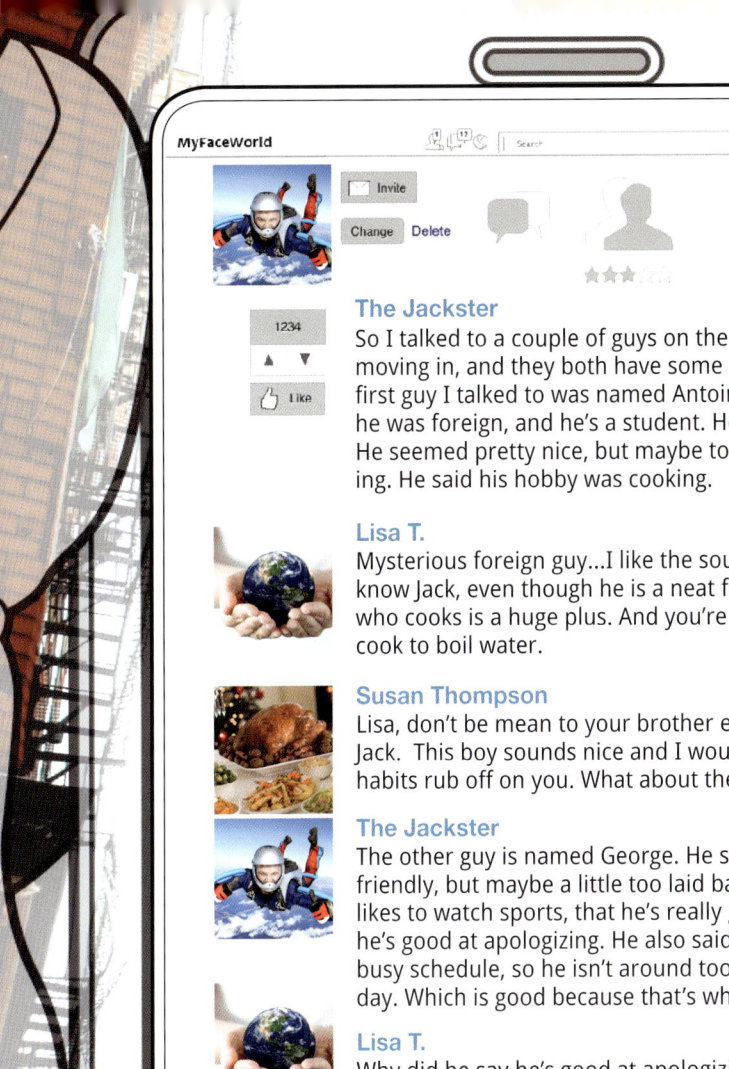

**The Jackster**
So I talked to a couple of guys on the phone today about moving in, and they both have some pros and cons. The first guy I talked to was named Antoine. He sounded like he was foreign, and he's a student. He had a slight accent. He seemed pretty nice, but maybe too strict about cleaning. He said his hobby was cooking.

**Lisa T.**
Mysterious foreign guy...I like the sound of that. You know Jack, even though he is a neat freak, a roommate who cooks is a huge plus. And you're not enough of a cook to boil water.

**Susan Thompson**
Lisa, don't be mean to your brother even though I agree. Jack. This boy sounds nice and I would hope some of his habits rub off on you. What about the other roommate?

**The Jackster**
The other guy is named George. He seemed really friendly, but maybe a little too laid back. He told me he likes to watch sports, that he's really generous, and that he's good at apologizing. He also said he has a really busy schedule, so he isn't around too much during the day. Which is good because that's when I usually sleep.

**Lisa T.**
Why did he say he's good at apologizing? It sounds like he could be a little too wild.

**The Jackster**
He told me that when he has his buddies over they get too loud, but he's good at apologizing to the neighbors. And that if he forgets to clean the dishes he gets to it eventually.

**Susan Thompson**
Jack, he doesn't sound responsible enough. He might be really friendly. He also might be lazier than you although he does have a job. Did he say he could pay the deposit?

**The Jackster**
Well, he said he lost his wallet, but that if I paid the deposit he would pay me right back. He does sound a little too relaxed. Even though Antoine sounds a little too neat, he did say he had every video game system ever made. That's pretty cool!

## A. Discussion

1. What things make an ideal roommate?
   ▸ What's the best number of people to live with? How many is too many?

2. What compromises do people need to make when living together?
   ▸ What are some things you do that might bother a roommate if you had one?

## B. Writing

Write a response to Jack telling him which roommate he should choose. Give him reasons why and some advice on how to live with that person.

## WARM UP

**Do you agree or disagree with the following statements? Why or why not?**

> The older you are the easier it is to get left behind by technology.
>
> Handwritten letters are pointless.
>
> We are currently living in the greatest period of change in history.
>
> Newer is always better.

### IDIOMS

- **Behind the times**
  My dad is really *behind the times*. He's been using the same cell phone for twelve years.
- **Cutting-edge**
  I heard she got a job with a really *cutting-edge* tech company.

### PHRASAL VERBS

- **Keep up**
- **Fall behind**
  The software updates are so fast these days that it's really hard to *keep up*. I've *fallen behind* recently.

### COLLOCATIONS

- **Computer illiterate**
  My grandmother is *computer illiterate*. She has no idea what email even is.
- **Tech savvy**
  My grandfather, on the other hand, is really *tech savvy*. He even builds his own robots.

# LESSON 1

## A. What's Old is New

- Comparatives and superlatives
- Advice with could and should

| STUDENT A |
|---|
| Film Camera |
| Word Processor |
| Landline Phone |
| Handwritten letters |
| Satellite/Cable TV |
| Microwave |
| Map and Compass |
| Text Messaging |
| CD Player |
| Books |

## PART 1

You and your partner are both using different types of technology. One of you is using **outdated** technology, and the other is using cutting-edge technology. In each case, try to explain to your partner why your type of technology is better, and persuade your partner to use the same technology as you.

> **Example:**
> **A:** *Film cameras are better than digital cameras because they allow you to be more creative.*
> **B:** *No....I think digital cameras are easier to use because they allow you to take as many pictures as necessary to get a good photo. Film is expensive! You should definitely buy a digital camera.*

| STUDENT B |
|---|
| Digital Camera |
| Typewriter |
| Mobile Phone |
| Email |
| TV on a Smart Phone/Tablet |
| Oven |
| Navigation System/GPS |
| Talking on the Phone |
| MP3 Player |
| E-books |

**outdated** *(adj.)*: behind current trends

## B. Postmodern Prometheus

### Pre-listening
- What jobs have robots taken away from people?
- Look at the picture and make a prediction about what kinds of things you think the robot can do.

### Listening  TRACK 18-19

Grandpa Charles built a robot! Find out what it can do!

### Post-listening

1 What three things does Grandpa say he has built the robot to do?

2 If you could build your own robot, what would it be able to do?

3 Do you know about any robots that are in use today? How are they used?

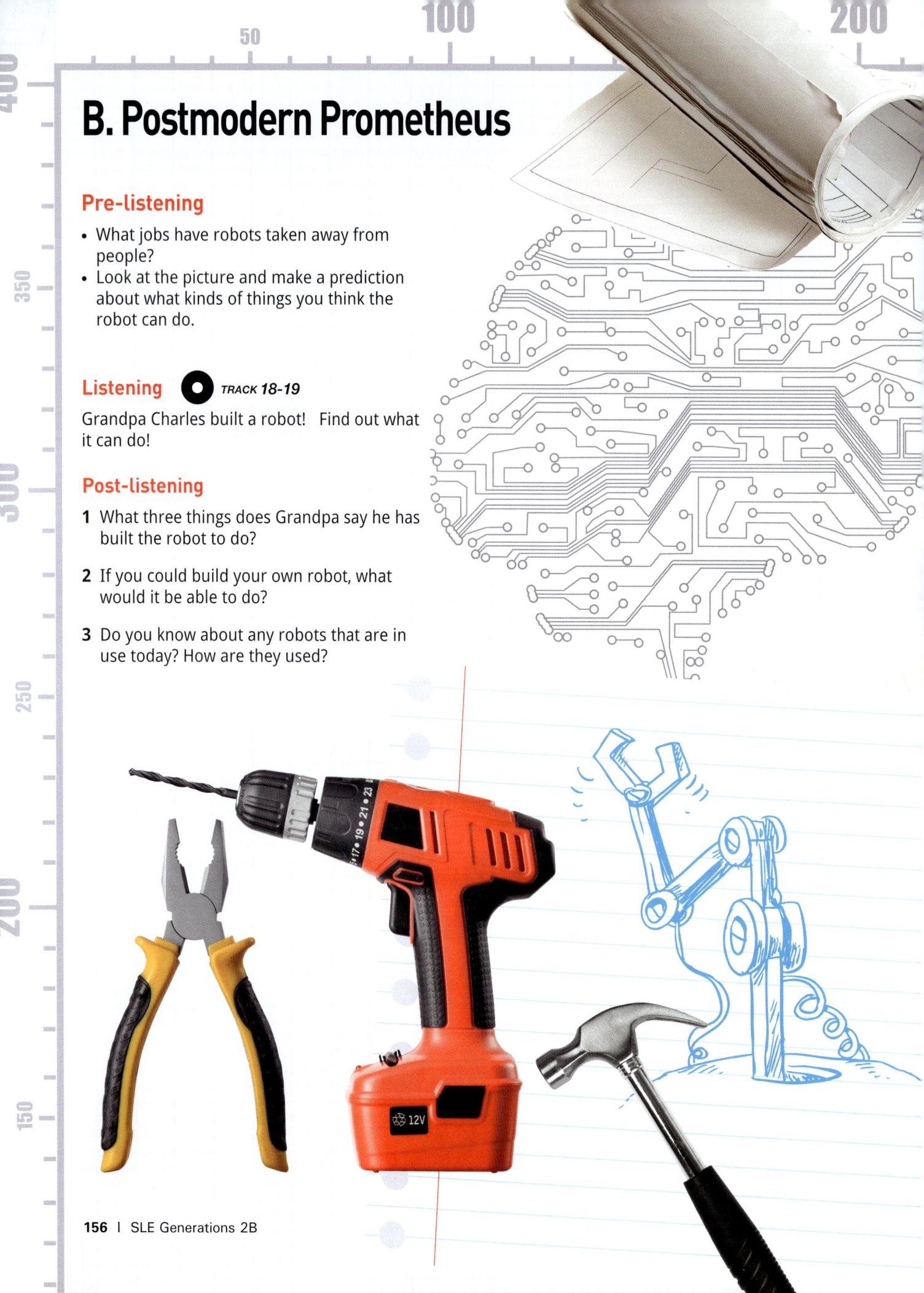

Unit 9 The Future is Now | 157

# C. Robot Schmobot

**PART 1** ● You have been given a very special opportunity! The JudsoCo Corporation™ has developed their first **humanoid** robot for personal home use. You have been selected to test out this robot, but first they want to know what kind of robot would be most useful to you.

**Step 1**

Functions. Below are a series of possible functions, but due to space and cost, only some can be put into your robot. A standard function is 1 point. An **upgraded** function is 3 points. Choose as many functions as you want up to a total of 10 points.

**Example:**
- *I want my robot to act as a life coach because I need someone to help me prepare for job interviews.*
- *I'd also like it if the robot could run errands and do all of my cleaning and laundry so I can have more free time to prepare for interviews.*
- *Finally, I want my robot to be able to give me a comforting hug because I need to get more hugs.*

**STANDARD** (1 point)

**UPGRADE** (3 points)

**1**

Standard ☐
The robot has limited speaking ability. It can use and understand 10 pre-programmed words.

Upgrade ☐
The robot has a vocabulary of 10,000 words.

**2**

Standard ☐
When you are not home, the robot can send the police a message if a **burglar** tries to enter.

Upgrade ☐
The robot will defend the home from **intruders**.

**3**

Standard ☐
The robot can make toast and coffee in the morning.

Upgrade ☐
The robot is a master cook and can create any meal you ask for.

**4**

Standard ☐
The robot can answer and open the front door.

Upgrade ☐
The robot can run **errands** for you.

---

**humanoid** *(adj.)*: having the appearance or characteristics of a human
**intruder** *(n.)*: someone who enters without permission
**burglar** *(n.)*: someone who enters a building illegally with the intent of stealing something
**errand** *(n.)*: a short trip with a clear goal or mission
**upgrade** *(v.)*: to improve

**5**

Standard ☐
The robot can give you a comforting hug.

Upgrade ☐
The robot can give you an excellent massage.

**6**

Standard ☐
The robot can **diagnose** minor health issues.

Upgrade ☐
The robot can **treat** minor health issues.

**7**

Standard ☐
The robot can give you fashion and style advice.

Upgrade ☐
The robot can act as a life coach and **therapist**.

**8**

Standard ☐
The robot can vacuum and clean up spills.

Upgrade ☐
The robot can do all of the cleaning and laundry in the house.

## Step 2

Select the appearance. Below are four possible body types. Discuss the pros and cons of the appearance of each. Which do you prefer and why?

## Step 3

Name your robot.

## Step 4

Present your robot!

*My robot's name is......*

**diagnose** *(v.)*: to determine the type of illness that someone has
**therapist** *(n.)*: someone who specializes in particular form of treatment
**treat** *(v.)*: to deal with or care for an illness or injury

## PART 2

You have had the robot for a few weeks. Below are a series of situations that have occurred in that time. Discuss how you and the robot you designed would handle the situations below.

1. You wake up and get ready for your day. What will you ask the robot to do?

2. You come home in the evening after a long day. What will you ask the robot to do?

3. You had a bad day. You got in a fight with your best friend.

4. You have an opportunity for a new job or promotion.

5. You've invited someone special to your house for a hot date. You really want to impress them.

6. It's late at night, and you hear someone break in.

7. You've been feeling feverish for a few days now. You've been really stressed with a few life issues, and you're not sure if that's causing it.

8. You are going on vacation for two weeks. What will you ask the robot to do while you are gone?

### Post questions:

1. Should robots look very little or very much like humans? Why?
2. Are there dangers in giving robots too much control over our lives?

# Discussion Questions

1. Do you think it's important to have the latest technological gadgets? Why or why not?
   - ▶ Would you consider yourself to be **tech savvy**?

2. Do you think it is possible to be **computer illiterate** and still be able to function in today's society? Why or why not?

3. What do you think are some of the factors that make it easy or difficult for people to adapt to new technology? Why?

4. How often do you use social networks, blogging, or message services?
   - ▶ What are some of the advantages and disadvantages of each?

5. How important do you think it is for older generations to adapt to new technology? Why?

6. If you could have some of the latest **cutting-edge** technology, which products would you choose?

7. Do you prefer to write by hand or to type? Why?

8. Does technology make us lazy?
   - ▶ Is that a good thing or a bad thing?

---

**computer literate** *(idiom)*: able to use and understand computers well
**cutting-edge** *(idiom)*: the most modern and advanced level of a thing or idea
**tech savvy** *(collocation)*: knowledgeable about technology

# LESSON 2

## >> WARM UP

**What do you think life will be like...**

...one year from today?
...ten years from today?
...a thousand years from today?

**Objectives:**
/ Discuss certainty about the future

# A. Perhaps One Day

| Less Certain (guessing) | More Certain (almost sure) | Very Certain (positive) |

| I **might** be able to invent a freeze ray. | I **could** invent a freeze ray, if I … | I **should** be able to invent a freeze ray. | I **wil**l invent a freeze ray and take over the world. |

## Degrees of Certainty about the Future

**PART 1**  Based on the situation, make a guess about the certainty of the following:

**Situation:**

The class starts in 10 minutes. I wonder who is coming.

- Josie texted that she's on the way.
- Nancy never misses class.
- Andy comes about half the time.
- Carl is in China on business. Who will and who won't be here?

**Situation:**

Next week, Jim is taking a vacation.

- He doesn't like getting wet.
- He has a picture of a camel on his computer screen.
- He enjoys spicy food.
- He speaks **fluent** Mongolian. Where is Jim going on his next vacation?

**Situation:**

I wonder what Mom's cooking for dinner?

- She said that she went to the store to buy meat.
- Grandpa can't eat beef because of his heart condition.
- It's Jack's birthday and he loves meatloaf.
- There's a recipe that calls for ground turkey on the kitchen counter. What will Susan cook for dinner?

**fluent** *(adj.)*: smooth, clear, and accurate

# PART 2

What is the certainty of these things happening in the next 10, 20, or 100 years?

**Example:**

Food Replicator

**A:** *We **won't be** able to design a machine that can make food in the next twenty years.*

**B:** *It **might be** possible if it worked like a printer. It **could** mix ingredients together.*

- Hover car
- Cure for common cold
- Flexible smart phones
- Laser weapons!
- Teleport machine
- Universal translator (can understand any language)
- Domed cities
- Force fields
- Time machine
- Levitation device
- Being able to choose your babies' features
- Living for an exceptionally long time
- **Bionic** body parts

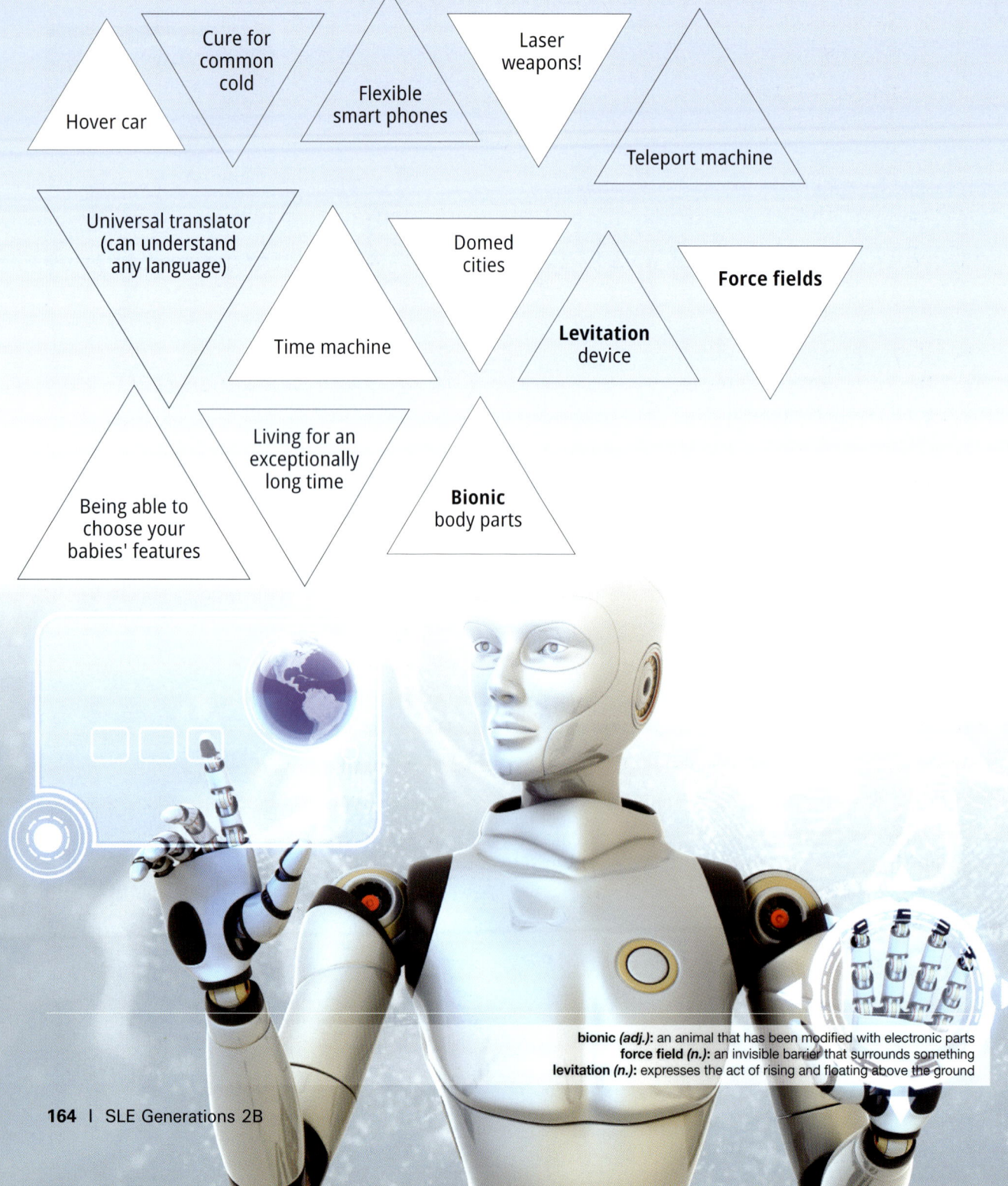

**bionic** *(adj.)*: an animal that has been modified with electronic parts
**force field** *(n.)*: an invisible barrier that surrounds something
**levitation** *(n.)*: expresses the act of rising and floating above the ground

# B. Time Keeps on Tickin'

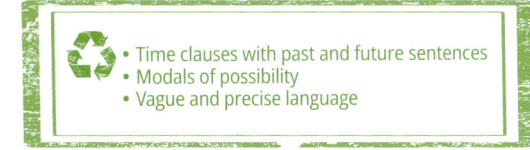

- Time clauses with past and future sentences
- Modals of possibility
- Vague and precise language

A. First pet
B. Learn to swim/ride a bike
C. Start school
D. First date
E. Graduate high school
F. First work experience
G. First trip with friends
H. Graduate university

I. Big trip abroad
J. Start career
K. Get married
L. Buy a house
M. Have a child
N. Become a grandparent
O. Retire
P. Other?

40yrs.  20yrs.  10yrs.  NOW  10yrs.  20yrs.  40yrs.

## PART 1

Place the important milestones above that have already happened for you along the timeline and compare them with others.

**Example:**

**A:** *I learned to swim before I started school.*
**B:** *Really? How old were you?*
**A:** *I was about four or five. How about you?*
**C:** *After I started school, I learned to swim.*
**B:** *Where did you go to school?*

## PART 2

Now make guesses about when the other milestones might happen in your life.

**Example:**

**A:** *I might go on a big trip abroad before I graduate university.*
**B:** *Where will you go?*
**A:** *I could go to Australia or New Zealand. What will you do?*
**C:** *I will buy a house after I get married.*

### Do You Remember?

When comparing times in the future the verb that comes after time words like *after*, *before*, and *when* must be in the simple present.

**Incorrect:**
I will buy a house after I **will** get married.
**Correct:**
I will buy a house after I get married.

Unit 9 The Future is Now | 165

# C. The Best Idea in History

- Superlatives and comparatives
- Unlikely situations

| | | | | |
|---|---|---|---|---|
| Airplane | Alphabet | Aspirin | Batteries | Chocolate |
| Car | Cell Phone | Credit Card | GPS | Internet |
| Dynamite | Guns | Light Bulb | Music | Nuclear Power |
| Television | Toilet | Video Games | Refrigerator | Toothbrush |

**PART 1** • For each category, discuss which invention deserves the award for _____.

1. Most likely to cause health problems
2. Most useful when dealing with the opposite sex
3. Least valuable
4. Most damaging to social skills
5. Most helpful in an emergency
6. Most harmful to the environment
7. Most underappreciated
8. Most useful on a desert island
9. Invention that shouldn't have been invented
10. Most addictive
11. Most versatile
12. Most likely to disappear in the future

**PART 2** • How would the world be different without these inventions?
What would change?
What would you do if they didn't exist?

# Discussion Questions

1. What are the pros and cons of owning a cell phone?
   - ▶ Do you think that cell phones ultimately improve people's lives?
   - ▶ Is it hard to **keep up** with the latest cell phone developments?

2. Would you rather communicate using only electronic communication devices (telephone, email, text message), or live with no form of electronic communication?

3. Which would you rather use for day-to-day transportation: a bicycle or a car?

4. What are some effects that **falling behind** can have on someone's life?
   - ▶ Do you know anyone who is **behind the times**? Is that person's life difficult because of it?

5. What types of technology are most important in modern society?
   - ▶ Can you think of any technology that's unnecessary?
   - ▶ What, in your opinion, is the greatest technological change of the past ten years? Why?

6. What future event are you most **looking forward to**?
   - ▶ When will this event happen?

7. What do you think I (your partner) will do tomorrow? Try to guess.

## UNIT 9 REVIEW

**How well can you use:**
- ☐ Expressions about technology?
- ☐ Expressing future certainty?

What do you need to study more?

---

**behind the times** *(idiom)*: describes someone that is not following current trends
**fall behind** *(phrasal verb)*: to be unable to follow the another's pace
**keep up** *(phrasal verb)*: to maintain the current level of something
**look forward to** *(phrasal verb)*: to anticipate something

## Activity: The World Future Grant

Your city has received a $20,000,000 "World Future" grant to develop local infrastructure. The city government is now accepting proposals. Decide which changes to the list are most important, and develop a proposal to present to the mayor (your teacher).

### Education:
- Provide scholarships to Engineering students in the city's most prestigious university: $6,000,000
- Develop a free computer-literacy program open to all of the city's residents: $6,000,000
- Provide a laptop for every student in local schools: $3,000,000

### Sustainability:
- Install solar panels on major buildings throughout the city: $7,000,000
- Construct community gardens in neighborhoods throughout the city: $5,000,000
- Start a citywide recycling program that requires all businesses to recycle: $5,000,000
- Purchase hybrid cars for all of the city's emergency forces: $1,000,000

### Health/wellness:
- Renovate the city's animal shelter to house a larger number of animals: $2,000,000
- Create a large public park in the downtown area: $1,000,000

### Entertainment/Communication:
- Build a new shopping mall with cutting-edge technology to attract tourists from around the world: $7,000,000
- Install citywide free wifi: $1,000,000

### Transportation:
- Build a new solar-powered sky train in the city's downtown area: $5,000,000
- Change the city's current public transportation system to improve safety features: $5,000,000
- Expand the public transportation system to reach new parts of the city: $5,000,000
- Widen roadways to reduce traffic congestion: $3,000,000

# Mysterious Robot Creates Panic and Prosperity

By **Lawson D. Woods**, PNN

The local community is in an uproar over a mysterious robot that has been seen going from neighborhood to neighborhood causing chaos. While many think he could be dangerous, he is quickly becoming a hero to people he has met.

Several members of the community have had firsthand experience with the robot, whose body seems to be made of household appliances.

Angie Moss, a landlady for many apartments in the area, described her encounter. "That robot destroyed my bathroom wall! And then he did my hair. It's never looked better! Maybe I should ask him to do it again."

"I tried to stop him," says house owner Dave Davidson. "I hit him with a broom. He looked at me and asked, 'Just what do you think you're doing, Dave?' I told him I was trying to get him to leave my house, that's what!" When Davidson then attempted to force the robot to leave, the robot replied, "I'm sorry Dave, I'm afraid I can't do that. There is still a large wine stain on your wife's blouse."

Davidson's wife finished by saying, "Even though my living room has been destroyed, he did a really good job getting those pesky stains out!"

Another local, Cathy Clutz, came home from work to discover the robot cooking a twelve-course meal in her kitchen. "There were pots and pans everywhere!" exclaimed Clutz. "It was a mess!" Once the robot had finished preparing the dinner, he gently gave Clutz a back massage and tucked her into bed. "I have to admit, it was one of the most romantic evenings I've had in a long time. I told him he should call me sometime!" said Clutz.

No one knows where the mysterious robot came from, but we know where he will be going in the future. According to a MyFaceWorld advertisement, he will be performing at the New Motive Power Jazz Café this Thursday at 8pm.

## A. Discussion

1. What kinds of things did the robot do to and for members of the community? Do you think the robot was more harmful or helpful? Why do you think so?
2. What are the pros and cons of having other people do things for you?
3. Do you think music created by technology (like computer software) should be considered the same as music created by people playing instruments?

## B. Writing

Write at least a paragraph telling the story from the perspective of another person who met the robot. What damage did it do? Then, how did it help?

# 10
# Looking Back
## Bringing It All Together

**Objectives:**
/ Review language points from previous chapters
/ Evaluate our progress
/ Work on communication and decision making skills

# WARM UP

**LANGUAGE POINTS SELF EVALUATION:**

Look at the following list of topics and skills covered throughout the book. Which topics and skills do you feel comfortable using? Which ones could you review?

**Unit 1** Hobbies and Free Time
- ☐ **Use to** and **Didn't use to** for talking about past habits.
- ☐ **Go + verb + ing** and **Go + to**

**Unit 2** Vague and Precise
- ☐ Using vague and precise expressions to describe situations.
- ☐ Prepositions of time.

**Unit 3** Rumors and Misunderstandings
- ☐ Checking and confirming information.
- ☐ Resolving misunderstandings.

**Unit 4** Social and Global Problems
- ☐ Expressing different levels of importance with modal verbs.
- ☐ **Even though** and **Although** to express contrast.

**Unit 5** Nonverbal Communication and Defining Characteristics
- ☐ Nonverbal communication.
- ☐ **Who, Which,** or **That** used to describe or define things and people.

**Unit 6** Past Speculations and Regrets
- ☐ Degrees of certainty about the past.
- ☐ Expressing regrets.

**Unit 7** Culture and Nation Building
- ☐ Expressing **dos** and **don'ts**.
- ☐ Using **adverbs**, **reasons**, and **time** with **imperatives**.

**Unit 8** Pros, Cons, and Contrasts
- ☐ Talking about living situations.
- ☐ Complaining and contrasting.

**Unit 9** Future Speculations and Technology
- ☐ Discussing technology.
- ☐ Degrees of certainty about the future.

### Evaluation

**3** = confident using this skill and will use it in the future.
**2** = need practice but have an overall understanding of the skill.
**1** = need to work on skill further to feel confident.

**42-54 points:** Ready for the next level, 2C.
**30-42 points:** Could move on to 2C, but might consider more study in 2B to become accurate.
**18-30 points:** Need further study in 2B to master skills.

# LESSON 1

## A. Design Your Own Apartment!

- Vague/precise amounts
- Even though/although
- Pros and cons

**PART 1**

You have wanted your own home for a long time. Finally, your home loan has been approved and you can move into your house next week.

- You have $15,000 to spend on new furniture.
- Look over the lists of items below and discuss what things you could live without, and the ones you think are necessities.
- Develop a final plan for the ideal home with your group.

### Appliances and electronics:
- Vacuum: $258
- Home computer: $1,958
- New heater/air conditioner: $2,630
- Dishwasher: $776
- Microwave: $338
- Toaster oven: $254
- Home theater system: $1689

### Furniture:
- Leather sofa: $1,450
- Armchair: $830
- Minibar: $750
- Dining room set: $1,295
- Bookcase: $450

### Indoor fixtures:
- New carpet: $1,880
- New paint/wallpaper: $1,549

### Bathroom Fixtures:
- Toilet paper dispenser: $28
- Shower/bathtub: $3,500
- Jacuzzi bathtub: $3,000
- Sauna: $2,395
- Toothbrush holder: $34
- Medicine cabinet and mirror: $289
- Full-length mirror: $195

### Bedroom:
- King size bed: $1,956
- Bunk beds for children: $970
- Dresser: $665
- Wardrobe: $2,250
- Vanity: $364

### Miscellaneous:
- Fireplace: $1,450
- House plants: $88
- Ping Pong table: $1,545

### PART 2

As you start to plan your new home, you discover some problems that need to be resolved in the house. Do you need to make any changes to your plan?

- The home's current carpet is covered with stains and has a strong, unpleasant odor.
- All of the walls inside the house are painted black.
- The kitchen has a stove but no oven.
- The shower in the only bathroom in the house does not work.
- The home has no heater or air conditioner.

Unit 10 Looking Back | 173

# B. Caketastrophe

- General amounts with fractions and percentages

## Pre-listening

Lisa and her friends are having a bake sale at their university to raise money for charity. Each day they have started with around ten cakes.

- Based on the information how many do you think they might have sold on each day?
- On which day did they sell more cakes? Why?

How many do you think they might sell today?

**Monday** –
*Weather:* hot and sunny
*Campus events:* Diet Club meeting
*Variables:* One third of the cakes melted in the sun.

**Tuesday** –
*Weather:* cool and rainy
*Campus events:* Football Club meeting
*Variables:* 25% of the cakes got wet.

**Today** – Started with exactly ten cakes.
*Weather:* hot and sunny
*Campus events:* new student registration and **faculty** meeting
*Variables:* Jack is bringing three extra cakes. Mary is bringing four more.

## Listening  TRACK 20-21

Hold up ten fingers and close your eyes. Take away or add fingers based on the information you hear. At the end of the listening, open your eyes and compare your results.

## Post-listening

1. Exactly how many cakes did Lisa have left?
2. Have you ever held an event to raise money?
   - If yes, what did you sell or what service did you provide?
   - If not, what do you think would be a good way to raise money?

**Bonus Question:**

Precisely how many cakes did Lisa sell?

**faculty** *(n.):* the collective group of teachers at an educational institution

# C. Taking Money from a Baby

**PART 1**

Look at the picture. One person will be the bank teller, the other group will be bank customers.

Look at your role card. Do NOT look at the other group's cards.

### Role Card: Bank Clerk

Be polite and serve the customer. Try to answer any questions that the customers ask.

**Bank Information**
1. The bank is open from 9 a.m. until 5 p.m., from Monday to Friday.
2. The afternoon is the busiest time. There are the fewest customers in the middle of the morning.
3. Apart from the money used by the bank clerks, all the money is stored in the vault. A secret code is needed to open the vault, and only the manager and the administrator know the secret code.
4. There is a button underneath the administrator's desk which starts an alarm ringing and calls the police.
5. The manager has a gun in the drawer of his desk.

**New accounts**
1. Ask for the customer's name and address.
2. Ask for two types of identification.
   (e.g. driver's license, passport, birth certificate, marriage certificate, etc.)
3. Take the customer's money.
4. Give the customer a new bank card.

**Deposits**
Take the customer's deposit slip.
OR
Help the customer fill in the deposit slip with: name, account number, amount, signature.
Take the customer's money.

**Withdrawals**
Similar to deposits

**Foreign exchange rate**
The bank will buy: £1.00 (British Pounds) for US $1.51
₩1,000 (Korean Won) for US $1.00

### Role Card: Customer(s)

You are planning to rob the bank. Each day, you will ask the bank clerk a different question. Ask *carefully*, otherwise the bank clerk might become suspicious! Take notes on what you find out.

**Monday**
1. Open an account.
2. Ask if all the money is stored in the vault.

**Tuesday**
1. Deposit $120 (ask the clerk to fill out the deposit slip for you).
2. Ask who can open the vault.

**Wednesday**
1. Ask for your account balance.
2. Withdraw $45 (ask the bank clerk to fill out the withdrawal slip for you).
3. Ask if there are any alarms in the bank.

**Thursday**
1. Change ₩50,000 into United States Dollars.
2. Ask when the bank is the most busy and least busy.

**Friday**
1. Ask for your account balance.
2. Deposit a check for $99 (ask the bank clerk to fill in the deposit for you).
3. Ask if there are any weapons in the bank.

SAVINGS ACCOUNT PASS BOOK

## PART 2

Why were the customers asking strange questions about the bank? Because they were planning to rob the bank! Now form small groups and plan the robbery based on your knowledge of the bank and the picture of the bank. Try to plan the robbery in as much detail as possible.

- Decide what time to rob the bank, and how the robbery will take place.
- Decide what each member of your group will do during the robbery.
- Choose a car and any three of the items below.

- Suggestions with could and should
- Superlatives and comparisons
- Prepositions of time

**Choose the vehicle:**

**Choose any THREE items:**

- A large bag
- A stun gun
- Masks
- A rope
- A handgun
- A trumpet
- A police uniform
- Dynamite
- A knife

When you have made your plan, present it to the rest of the class. Ask each other questions and decide which group made the best plan.

# D. Comedy of Errors

Divide into teams. One team should flip a coin to move to a square (heads: one space, tails: two spaces). After landing on a space, change the incorrect sentence into a correct sentence, or follow the direction. A correct answer is worth 3 points. The next team flips the coin to move forward. The team with the most points at the end of the game wins!

| START | I went to ski on the weekend. | I put on the bus near my home. | I going Japan for vacation. | I started working for this company for two years. | My grandfather was died. |
|---|---|---|---|---|---|
| I can't ride a horse. -Me too. | I was drunken last night. | Aren't you tired? -No, I'm tired. | I didn't used to have long hair. | I have my teeth check by a dentist. | About 72.3 percent of the class is female. |
| Do you got a pen I could borrow? | He's best singer in the class. | My birthday is at February in the second. | This shirt was made by India. | I heard that you go to a good café last night. | I have many free times. |
| You work at home, don't you? -Yes, I don't. | **Answer this question:** How many coffees/copies do you make every day? | Would you rather to go shopping or skating? | You could go to the hospital if you have a broken leg. | **Say this number:** 591,006,060 | I don't smoke. -neither can I. |
| Even though I am a child, I don't work. | I am confusing about that. | An athlete is a person which has to train very hard. | I would call if I have a phone. | I must have left my phone at home because I hear a buzzing in my bag. | I have ever had a car crash. |
| I have been waited in line for three hours! | I'm thirsty. I should have drunken some water. | I sometimes arrive lately. | When you visit my country, you don't keep your shoes on in the house. | I don't never go to the library. | I'm not too wealthy to buy a car, even though I saved a lot of money. |
| I'll cook dinner while I come home. | The disadvantage of city life are all the traffics. | **Say this number:** 13,131,001 | Mails are the worst way to send information. | I cut my hair at the salon. | Could you tell me when does finish class. |
| FINISH | I feel flu and have dizzy. | I will buy a house after I will get married. | Do you know she is smart? | The world might been hotter ten years in the future. | He went to the movie with himself. |

**direction** *(n.)*: instruction or command

# E. Review Discussion

Let's discuss what has happened to the Thompson family so far and talk about ourselves.
Give reasons for your answers, and ask follow up questions.

1. What did Grandpa use to do when he was younger?
   ▶ What is an activity you used to do but don't anymore?
2. What activities would you like to try, and where would you go to try them?

3. What kind of job did Jack start in order to raise money?
   ▶ How much money does a person need to move out and get their own place?
4. What month and season were you born in? What day were you born on? What time of day?

5. What is something Jack heard Grandma Martha say that caused a misunderstanding?
   ▶ Has anyone told you something that you misunderstood?
6. What things cause confusion when speaking English? How can you clear up these misunderstandings?

7. What emergency did the family face?
   ▶ What is the worst personal emergency you have faced?
8. What is something you had to continue doing even though you wanted to give up?

9. What kind of T.V. shows does Susan like watching? How about Richard?
   ▶ How do you show someone you like or dislike a T.V. show without speaking?
10. Who is a person that has had a strong influence on your life? How about a thing?

11. How many continents was Mr. Squiggles seen on?
    ▶ Which continent would you most like to visit?
12. What do you regret not doing on a past trip you took?

13. Where is Lisa going on her trip?
    ▶ Have you ever been to Europe? Would you like to go to Europe? Where?
14. What are some cultural dos and don'ts when visiting those places?

15. How many people does Jack interview as potential roommates?
    ▶ Would you rather live by yourself or with a roommate? Why?
16. What's a problem with your living situation, and what's good about it?

17. What happened to Grandpa's robot? What did it do?
    ▶ When do you think we will have robots for our own personal use?
18. What will you be doing at this time next week?

19. What predictions could you make about the Thompson family?
    ▶ Where will they go and what will they do?
20. What are your plans for studying English? What will you do next?

# Activity: Tour Guide

A group of foreign tourists is visiting your hometown this weekend, and the government has asked you to serve as a tour guide! Work with a partner to plan a three-day itinerary for the group.

- Vague and Precise language
- Prepositions of time
- Two actions happening at the same time
- Suggestions with could and should

**Some notes:**

**Activities:**
- The group wants to experience the culture of your country.
- The group is expecting three activities per day: one in the morning, one in the afternoon, and one in the evening.
- The group does not want to do the same activity twice.
- The group has requested at least one of each of the following types of activities:
  > Educational
  > Recreational
  > Dancing/singing
  > Shopping
  > Outdoor

**Food:**
- The group wants to sample a variety of food from your country.
- The group does not want to eat the same kind of food more than twice.
- One of the group members is vegetarian.

### Example:

**A:** *Let's make sure that we take the group to the beach on the first morning! The beach is so beautiful in the spring.*

**B:** *While we're there, we can eat grilled seafood.*

**C:** *After lunch we could take them to the aquarium. It's around that area.*

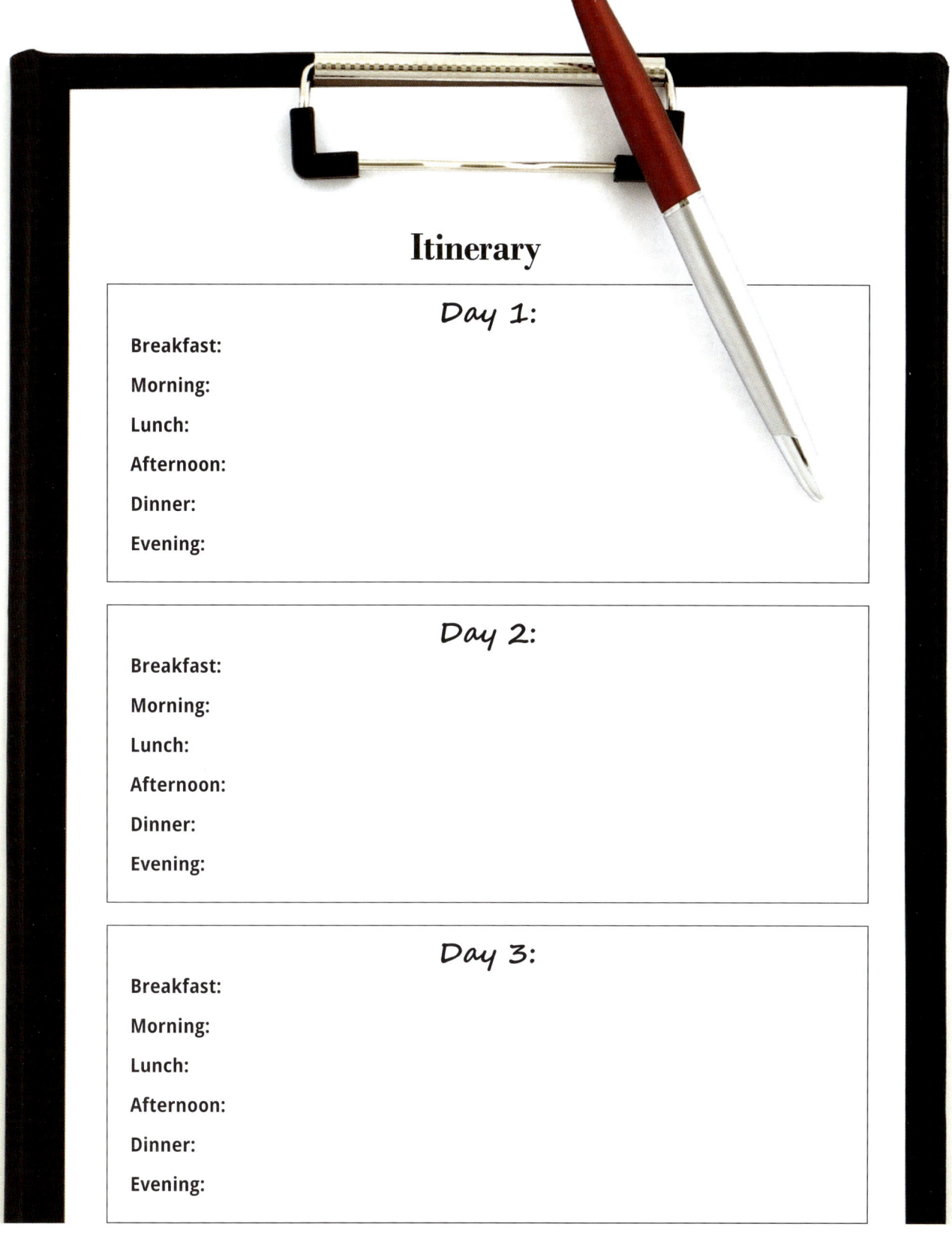

**Challenge:**

- On Day 1, you find out that one of the group members is allergic to shellfish. Do you need to do anything to help them?
- On Days 2 and 3, it's raining. Do you need to change any of your plans, or can you help the group find the silver lining?

# LISTENING DIALOGUES SLE 2B

## UNIT 1  TRACK 2 and 3

**Charles:** What's that horrible noise? Is the cat crying?

**Lisa:** No, Grandpa, that's just Jack's music.

**Charles:** Music? I can't hear any music. Maybe my hearing aid is broken. I just hear a lot of static and pops.

**Lisa:** Grandpa, that IS the music.

**Charles:** Kids these days. Back in my day, musicians actually played instruments. How are you supposed to dance to this?

**Lisa:** Ha, you dance, Grandpa?

**Charles:** Now, Lisa, I didn't use to be this old, you know. We were all young once.

**Lisa:** I know. But it's hard to imagine you in your twenties.

**Charles:** You should have seen your father when he was your age.

**Lisa:** I can't imagine that either!

**Charles:** Oh, he would get into all kinds of trouble.

**Lisa:** Really? Like what?

**Charles:** Oh, now, I don't know if I should…

**Lisa:** Come on, Grandpa…

**Charles:** Okay. Just one story. Now your father used to LOVE blueberries. One day, your grandmother had baked one of her famous blueberry pies. She has always loved cooking. Well, your father, he was maybe eight years old, he snuck into the kitchen and ate the ENTIRE thing. All by himself.

**Lisa:** The whole thing?

**Charles:** Yes, and when we asked him about it, he said he didn't do it. Even though his face was covered in blueberries! He tried to blame the family cat! Can you believe it? Oh, he got SO sick.

**Lisa:** That's amazing!

**Charles:** After that, we called him our Little Piggy. He hated it.

**Richard:** He hated what? What are you talking about?

**Lisa:** Oh, hey, Little Piggy…I mean Dad.

**Richard:** Little Pi…wait… Dad, you didn't tell her THAT story?

**Charles:** What? She asked. Besides, I didn't tell her anything TOO embarrassing, like about how you used to…

**Richard:** Whoa, whoa, whoa, that's enough of that!

# UNIT 2  TRACK 4 and 5

**Jack:** Mom, Dad, I've finally got a job!

**Susan:** That's great, Jack!

**Richard:** About time!

**Susan:** So what is it?

**Jack:** Err…it's…I uh…kind of a management position.

**Susan:** Oooh, sounds fancy.

**Richard:** Managing what, exactly?

**Jack:** Managing…well, it's sort of a music industry thing.

**Richard:** Uh huh. And this "sort of" music industry job, does it pay well?

**Jack:** Well…ish.

**Richard:** What does that mean?

**Jack:** Okay, maybe it doesn't pay yet, but…

**Susan:** It doesn't pay?!

**Richard:** Jack, specifically: what is this job?

**Jack:** I've offered to be the band manager for the Crimson Kings.

**Susan:** You mean your friend Paul's little group?

**Jack:** Mom, they're great! They're going to be huge! And they need somebody to help them organize and plan for events and stuff.

**Richard:** I thought you were trying to raise money so you could move into your own apartment.

**Jack:** Yeah.

**Susan:** And how will you make money doing this?

**Jack:** I…well…I guess…I don't know.

**Richard:** I suggest you find another way to make money. We told you earlier – if you save at least half of the amount needed to rent an apartment, we will pay the other half. You're not going to get that money helping your friend's band. Have you saved any money?

**Jack:** Around twenty bucks.

**Richard:** That's not even close. So until you have that money, you'll have to keep doing your chores. Now go clean the garage.

**Jack:** Okay, okay…


# UNIT 3  TRACK 6 and 7

**Martha:** Can you give me a hand, Jack?

**Jack:** Yeah, Grandma, they were great!

**Martha:** What, Jack? I don't understand. I asked for a hand. I meant I need some help.

**Jack:** Oh, sorry! I just got back from a concert. I thought I heard you ask about the band. Maybe it was a little loud – I think I'm having troubles with my ears.

**Martha:** Now, Jack, you shouldn't be drinking so much.

**Jack:** Drinking? Grandma, I said "EARS", not BEERS.

**Martha:** Oh, ha. Maybe my hearing is not so great either.

**Jack:** So what did you need a hand with?

**Martha:** Oh, that's right. Your mom told me you needed to earn some money.

**Jack:** Yeah?

**Martha:** I will give you five whole dollars if you wash the cat.

**Jack:** Five dollars just to look at the cat?

**Martha:** No, no, you need to clean the cat. Scrub-a-dub-dub.

**Jack:** Oh, I understand! Sure, I guess I can do that. But doesn't the cat hate baths?

**Martha:** No, I don't think so.

**Jack:** If you say so! I'll go do it now! Come on, Mr. Squiggles.

**Martha:** Why on Earth would a cat hate maths?

**Jack:** Ow…ow….ow….

**Martha:** Wait. Did he say baths or maths? Oh, dear.

# UNIT 4  TRACK 8 and 9

**Richard:** That was the water department on the phone.

**Susan:** Did they say we have to evacuate?

**Richard:** They said that we don't have to evacuate yet, but that we should prepare to leave if the water gets closer to the house.

**Susan:** Well we'd better start to pack the car in case we have to make an emergency exit.

**Richard:** Right. What are the most important things in the house?

**Susan:** Well, there's my family's quilt. I would hate not to be able to give that to Lisa.

**Richard:** Okay. I'll get my bowling trophy, those are hard to come by.

**Susan:** Oh, Richard. Couldn't you get the photo album instead? There's a picture in there of you with the trophy.

**Richard:** Fair enough. What about all the birth certificates, and diplomas, and……..

**Susan:** I've put all of those things in an envelope marked documents. It's in the drawer next to the…..

**Richard:** Computer! It's too big to bring. I'll back up everything onto a hard drive.

**Susan:** We have to bring the baby's special blanket.

**Richard:** And Jack should bring his guitar.

**Susan:** I could get the jewelry box.

**Richard:** We have to pack all of Mom's medication. We don't know how long we'll be gone.

**Susan:** It seems like we're forgetting something…………..What is it?

# UNIT 5  TRACK 10 and 11

**Lisa:** What are you watching, Dad?

**Richard:** I haven't decided yet. Let's see what's on TV.

**Richard:** Oh, this show is great.

**Lisa:** I don't want to watch anything with people in suits….this looks way too boring. I'd rather watch something fun and exciting.

**Richard:** This is the Daily Gag Report, Lisa. This man might not look entertaining because of his clothes, but he's actually one of the funniest comedians on television!

**Lisa:** Let's change the channel.

**Lisa:** What about this show?

**Richard:** I don't know, Lisa. Don't you think that girl looks a little irresponsible?

**Lisa:** Why would you say that?

**Richard:** Because she's not wearing a seatbelt!

**Lisa:** This is my favorite show…it's called SoCal Life.

**Richard:** Let's keep looking.

**Lisa:** Oh! Stop there!!

**Richard:** Now Lisa, I don't want to watch this. That guy seems a bit young and rebellious for my taste.

**Lisa:** Dad, I know that this guy looks like that because of his tattoos, but you won't believe who he is!

**Richard:** Is he a criminal? Is this some kind of crime drama?

**Lisa:** No dad, this is James Block, the famous Smithson University engineer who just invented a new, ultra-safe car.

**Richard:** Wow…this looks interesting. Let's watch it!


# UNIT 6  TRACK 12 and 13

**Jack:** Lisa, come here! Look at this!

**Lisa:** What is it?

**Jack:** You know how I made a website to help us find Mr. Squiggles a while back?

**Lisa:** Yeah. I wasn't sure if it would do any good. Any luck?

**Jack:** Actually, we have been getting posts from all over the world!

**Lisa:** What? How is that possible?

**Jack:** I don't know! Look at this one. This first picture was posted last week by a guy in Spain!

**Lisa:** You mean that picture of the beach?

**Jack:** Yeah. Ha, he looks so relaxed. Whoa, but look!

**Lisa:** Is that Mr. Squiggles with a…

**Jack:** …a lion! In Kenya! After Europe, he went to Africa!

**Lisa:** And there! A few days later. That picture with the elephant. He was in…Thailand! How did he get from Europe to Asia so quickly?

**Jack:** I don't know. But from there, he went hiking with some girl in Australia! It looks hot…

**Lisa:** No way! This next picture was posted by a group of scientists in…Antarctica?! Look at Mr. Squiggles! He's hanging out with a bunch of penguins! Can you believe it?

**Jack:** Next, there is Seňora Camila in…Brazil? She said she had a dance lesson with a mysterious cat who looks a lot like Mr. Squiggles.

**Lisa:** How is he doing it?

**Jack:** I don't know, but maybe we'll find out soon. Look! This most recent post! A group of tourists in Hollywood, California took this picture! They must have thought he was famous!

**Lisa:** Really? He's already made it all the way around the world?

**Jack:** Yeah. Who knows, maybe he'll find his way home soon!

# UNIT 7   TRACK 14 and 15

**Charles:** Lisa, I'm so happy that you are going on your first trip to Europe tomorrow! I remember my first trip to Europe…that was so long ago.

**Lisa:** Grandpa, I land in Paris at 2:00 PM on Friday. What's the first thing I should do?

**Charles:** Well Lisa, the most important tip I can give you is to travel cautiously so that you don't get lost or get into any trouble! Oh, and hold onto your passport tightly so you don't lose it!

**Lisa:** I know, I know, but what about the fun??

**Charles:** Since you're asking about fun, definitely go on a boat tour.

**Lisa:** How do I get there?

**Charles:** Always take the subway because it's cheaper. Carefully read the map because the subway is a bit confusing.

**Lisa:** Sounds good. What should I eat?

**Charles:** Absolutely eat some crepes on the street because they're cheap and delicious.

**Lisa:** Got it. What did you do for fun at night?

**Charles:** Read at night so you can save a little money!

**Lisa:** Seriously, Grandpa?

**Charles:** Well……I did hear about a cafe on the left bank where you can hear live jazz musicians.

**Lisa:** I'm going to check out that cafe!

**Charles:** Always go out with friends. Never walk on the streets alone, and don't talk to strangers!

**Lisa:** I'm not a little kid anymore! Please don't give me advice like that. I know!

**Charles:** Okay, okay, Lisa. But don't be in such a hurry to grow up…enjoy being young while you can…oh, and wear sunscreen!

**Lisa:** Got it. Thanks, grandpa.

# UNIT 8  TRACK 16 and 17

**Jack:** Hello?

**Antoine:** Hello, my name is Antoine. I'm calling in response to Jack's request for a roommate?

**Jack:** This is Jack. Thanks for calling! Tell me a little bit about yourself.

**Antoine:** Hmmm…I'm a student, so I spend a lot of time at home studying. I usually prefer to keep the music quiet so I can focus.

**Jack:** Oh….I see…

**Antoine:** One of my hobbies is cooking, so I like to cook healthy meals for people in my free time. Anyways, how do you feel about cleaning?

**Jack:** Uhhh…

**Antoine:** I think it's good to make a cleaning schedule so we can share the work.

**Jack:** Uh, yeah. So what do you do for fun?

**Antoine:** Oh yeah, fun. I have every video game system ever made.

**Jack:** Whoa, really?!

**Antoine:** So…what do you do?

**Jack:** I'm…kind of…part of a band.

**Antoine:** Oh…I see. Tell you what, I'll call you back…

**Jack:** Alright. Later!


**Jack:** Hello?

**George:** Hey. Can I speak to Jack?

**Jack:** This is Jack. How can I help you?

**George:** Jack! George! I'm calling in response to your ad seeking a roommate.

**Jack:** Oh, great! Tell me a little bit about yourself.

**George:** Well, I'm a friendly guy. I love to talk and hang out. I have friends over all the time at night to party, and of course you're welcome to hang out with us.

**Jack:** Wow, sounds great!

**George:** Yeah. Um…if my buddies are too loud, I'm good at apologizing to the neighbors. I'm a generous guy, so people like me. I'm totally okay with sharing everything in the fridge. What's mine is yours and what's yours is mine, right?

**Jack:** Well, I guess that might be okay…

**George:** When I'm not hanging out with my friends, I'm pretty busy with work. Since my schedule is full, it sometimes takes me a little while to clean, but I usually do it eventually.

**Jack:** That's good enough for me!

**George:** Oh…and um….can you pay my deposit? I lost my wallet and I need to go to the bank. I'll pay you back.

**Jack:** What? Ummm…can I call you back?

**George:** Sure, talk to you later.

# UNIT 9  TRACK 18 and 19

**Susan:** Hey, Dad. What are you up to?

**Charles:** Just putting the final touches on my robot, Bill. Say hello, Bill!

**Bill:** Hello, Bill.

**Susan:** Wow, that's really impressive. How did you do it?

**Charles:** Well, I used to be an engineer in my military days. Everything else I learned from the internet. I even bought the parts from a website. Next thing you know, I have Bill!

**Bill:** Hello, Bill.

**Susan:** What does it do?

**Charles:** Anything we want! With my remote control, I can tell Bill to do all kinds of things. Help with chores. Wash the cat. That kind of thing.

**Susan:** Really? That's incredible!

**Charles:** Yes, but…his main function is…

**Susan:** What, Dad?

**Charles:** It may sound a little silly, but I programmed him to play the trombone!

**Susan:** So now you have someone to play with! I think that's a great idea!

**Charles:** Let me show you how it…hey, where's my remote control?

**Charles:** Oh, Baby Jane, don't push that button!

**Bill:** Command accepted. Run, Bill. Run.

**Susan:** Oh my goodness! He just ran straight through the wall! Where is he going?

**Charles:** Bill? Bill, come back!

**Susan:** He's…it looks like he's gone, Dad.

**Charles:** This can't be good…


# UNIT 10  TRACK 20 and 21

**Lisa:** Mom, I need help! I'm at the bake sale and we need more cakes!

**Susan:** Really? Already?

**Lisa:** Yeah. We came to the sale with ten cakes, and we sold half of them within the first hour.

**Susan:** Didn't Jack bring more?

**Lisa:** Jack brought three more cakes, yeah. But then he dropped one of them and it went everywhere.

**Susan:** Oh no!

**Lisa:** We sold another cake an hour later. We didn't realize how hot it was outside and one third of the cakes melted in the sun. We couldn't sell them.

**Susan:** What a waste!

**Lisa:** Luckily, Mary came with more cakes. She doubled the number of cakes we had.

**Susan:** So you still have plenty?

**Lisa:** No! We sold one to a woman for her daughter's birthday, two more to a new student who is having a housewarming party and two to a professor for a faculty meeting.

**Susan:** It sounds like you are doing really well!

**Lisa:** Yeah, but when I took a break, Jack got hungry and ATE one of the cakes! All by himself!

**Susan:** So wait. I'm confused? Exactly how many cakes do you have?

# GLOSSARY SLE 2B

### A

**adverse** *adjective* negative, dangerous, harmful — Unit 9
**ambulance** *noun* a vehicle that is intended to transport people from and to a hospital facility — Unit 4
**an accident waiting to happen** *idiom* an expression used to describe a situation that will most likely lead to a problem or accident — Unit 4
**arcade** *noun* a place where people go to play video games that cost a penny each — Unit 1
**asteroid** *noun* a rock that orbits around the sun — Unit 4
**autograph** *noun* signature — Unit 2
**avalanche** *noun* snow suddenly falling down the side of a mountain — Unit 4

### B

**barter** *verb* to trade/exchange services or goods — Unit 8
**beat around the bush** *idiom* to avoid saying something by addressing other topics — Unit 2
**behind the times** *idiom* describes someone that is not following current trends — Unit 9
**better to be safe than sorry** *idiom* the idea that one should always try to be careful — Unit 4
**bionic** *adjective* an animal that has been modified with electronic parts — Unit 9
**blend in** *phrasal verb* to be difficult to distinguish from the surroundings — Unit 7
**blunt** *adjective* extremely straightforward with one's words and actions — Unit 4
**boutique** *noun* a small independently owned clothing shop. — Unit 1
**burglar** *noun* someone who enters a building illegally with the intent of stealing something — Unit 9
**BYOB** *adjective-slang* used to describe a party or event which guests are expected to bring their own beverages — Unit 2

### C

**censor** *verb* to restrict in order to prevent threats to security/authority — Unit 8
**chew over** *phrasal verb* to continue thinking about something after it is over — Unit 6
**chew someone out** *idiom* to scold someone — Unit 8
**chore** *noun* a task that one must do on a regular basis — Unit 1
**clear up** *phrasal verb* to resolve a misunderstanding — Unit 3
**client** *noun* a person or group that receives service or products — Unit 2
**compulsive** *adjective* driven by strong drive to do certain things — Unit 4
**computer literate** *idiom* able to use and understand computers well — Unit 9
**confirm** *verb* to verify a piece of true information — Unit 3
**consequence** *noun* result — Unit 6
**conservationism** *noun* the idea that protecting the environment is beneficial — Unit 4
**consumerism** *noun* belief in the idea that acquiring goods is positive and beneficial — Unit 4
**convenience** *noun* expresses the quality of being easy to use and comfortable — Unit 8
**conventional** *adjective* normal, typical, or in accordance with custom/tradition — Unit 9
**correct** *verb* to find and resolve an error/mistake — Unit 3
**crash** *idiom* to go home in order to go asleep — Unit 8
**culture shock** *noun* surprise felt from exposure to a new culture — Unit 7
**cutting edge** *idiom* the most modern and advanced level of a thing or idea — Unit 9

## D

**detail-oriented** *adjective* able to focus on the small aspects of a matter — Unit 2
**diagnose** *verb* to determine the type of illness that someone has — Unit 9
**direction** *noun* instruction or command — Unit 10
**discrimination** *noun* inequitable treatment of a person or group — Unit 7
**dormant** *adjective* not active — Unit 4
**downside** *noun* disadvantage — Unit 8
**drought** *noun* a period of water shortage — Unit 4
**duet** *noun* a musical piece performed by two musicians — Unit 2

## E

**errand** *noun* a short trip with a clear goal or mission — Unit 9

## F

**faculty** *noun* the collective group of teachers at an educational institution — Unit 9
**fall behind** *phrasal verb* to be unable to follow the another's pace — Unit 9
**figure out** *phrasal verb* to make sense of, to resolve — unit 5
**fire extinguisher** *noun* a device that stops a fire — Unit 4
**flea market** *noun* a market that sells used goods — Unit 1
**fluent** *adjective* smooth, clear, and accurate — Unit 9
**force field** *noun* an invisible barrier that surrounds something — Unit 9
**fortune teller** *noun* a person who attempts to predict others' futures — Unit 3

## G

**get across** *phrasal verb* to communicate or express information — Unit 5
**gig** *noun* a performance Unit 2
**give or take** *idiom* expresses approximate information — Unit 2
**go out** *phrasal verb* to spend time together outside of one's home — Unit 1
**go with the flow** *idiom* to do what other people are doing — Unit 7
**good judge of character** *idiom* able to decide whether someone is good or bad easily — Unit 5

## H

**hang out** *phrasal verb* to spend time together — Unit 1
**hiccups** *noun* sound made that effects one's breathing — Unit 4
**hindsight** *noun* the understanding gained after an incident has occurred — Unit 6
**hit** *adjective* extremely popular — Unit 5
**humanoid** *adjective* having the appearance or characteristics of a human — Unit 9

## I

**intruder** *noun* someone who enters without permission — Unit 9

## J

**jump to conclusions** *idiom* to make a quick decision — Unit 5
**junk food** *idiom* food that does not benefit a person's health — Unit 8

## K

**keep your cool** *idiom* to remain calm — Unit 4
**keep up** *phrasal verb* to maintain the current level of something — Unit 9

## L

**ladies' man** *noun* a man who attracts women — Unit 4
**landmark** *noun* a significant, easily recognizable feature or structure — Unit 1
**levitation** *noun* expresses the act of rising and floating above the ground — Unit 9
**lifeboat** *noun* a small boat that is kept on a larger boat in case of emergencies — Unit 6
**look back on (something)** *phrasal verb* to think about the past — unit 6
**look forward to** *phrasal verb* to anticipate something — unit 9
**look over** *phrasal verb* to visually scan something or someone — Unit 2
**lost in translation** *idiom* does not translate from one culture to another — Unit 3

## M

**morning person** *noun* a person who enjoys the morning — Unit 2
**mortician** *noun* someone who prepares a person's body after they have died — Unit 3
**move in** *phrasal verb* occupy a house — Unit 8
**move out** *phrasal verb* leave a house — Unit 8
**multitask** *verb* to do a variety of activities at the same time — Unit 8

## N

**natural disaster** *noun* a catastrophic event caused by forces of nature — Unit 4
**next-door neighbor** *noun* someone who lives in the home next to one's own home — Unit 8
**nickname** *noun* alternative name for someone or something — Unit 1
**night owl** *noun* a person who enjoys nighttime and thrives at this time — Unit 2

## O

**outbreak** *noun* the sudden spread of something such as sickness or conflict — Unit 4
**outdated** *adjective* behind current trends — Unit 9
**outdoorsy** *adjective* well suited to an outdoor environment — Unit 1

## P

**parasailing** *noun* a sport that involves pulling a person wearing a parachute above a boat — Unit 1
**pass time** *idiom* to do something with free time — Unit 1
**pick pocket** *noun* a thief who steals by taking an item out of someone's pocket — Unit 4
**poker face** *idiom* a face that expresses no emotion — Unit 5
**promote** *verb* to encourage people to purchase something — Unit 2
**put (someone) up** *phrasal verb* to allow a person to stay at one's home — Unit 8

## Q

**raffle** *noun* a contest in which players are assigned tickets, which are then selected at random `Unit 8`
**reliable** *adjective* someone or something that is there when you need it `Unit 5`
**roughly** *adverb* denotes that a number is not exact, but rather is an approximate estimation `Unit 2`
**round** *verb* to express a complex number by expressing the whole number above or below it `Unit 2`
**rumor** *noun* a piece of information that is spread around not supported by facts/data `Unit 3`
**rush hour** *noun* the period of time when people travel to and from work `Unit 2`

**scaredy cat** *idiom* a person who is easily frightened or intimidated `Unit 4`
**sidekick** *noun* a hero's assistant `Unit 5`
**sleep in** *phrasal verb* to sleep longer than is typical `Unit 2`
**slip one's mind** *idiom* to forget about something `Unit 6`
**sound** *adjective* stable and secure `Unit 7`
**speculate** *verb* to make a guess about something `Unit 6`
**spin doctor** *noun* a person who is able to present all information in a positive way `Unit 8`
**spot on** *phrasal verb* exactly correct `Unit 3`
**spread a rumor** *collocation* to tell a piece of unconfirmed information to other people `Unit 3`
**staycation** *idiom* a vacation that does not involve traveling `Unit 1`
**stick out** *phrasal verb* to be easy to distinguish from the surroundings `Unit 7`
**swamped** *idiom* extremely busy `Unit 1`

**table manner** *collocation* the way that a person acts while dining at a table `Unit 7`
**take a risk** *idiom* to do something without knowing what the result will be `Unit 4`
**take cover** *collocation* to seek out a safe and protective place during a dangerous situation `Unit 4`
**take off** *phrasal verb* to run away suddenly and quickly `Unit 4`
**take over** *phrasal verb* to assume power over something `Unit 4`
**take precautions** *collocation* to take steps to protect the safety of oneself `Unit 4`
**take something for granted** *idiom* to not appreciate the value of something `Unit 7`
**team-building** *adjective* intended to build relationships between the members of a group `Unit 2`
**tech savvy** *collocation* knowledgeable about technology `Unit 9`
**therapist** *noun* someone who specializes in particular form of treatment `Unit 9`
**tidal wave** *noun* a large wave from the ocean that causes destruction `Unit 4`
**tip** *verb* to give money in exchange for service `unit 7`
**tornado** *noun* air that moves over land and leaves destruction on the land that it touches `Unit 4`
**treat** *verb* to deal with or care for an illness or injury `Unit 9`

**under the wrong impression** *idiom* describes someone who is misinformed `Unit 3`
**upgrade** *verb* to improve `Unit 9`
**upside** *noun* advantage `Unit 8`

**vegan** *adjective* a person who does not believe in eating animal products `Unit 8`

Glossary | 193

**watch out** *phrasal verb* to be alert to a problem or danger  Unit 3
**what's done is done** *idiom* once something has been done, it cannot be changed  Unit 6
**whisk** *verb* to stir lightly  Unit 7
**word of mouth** *idiom* an expression used to describe spoken communication  Unit 3
**working holiday** *noun* going on holiday and working at the same time  Unit 3

**yawn** *verb* to open one's mouth and take a big breath  Unit 5

# NOTE

# NOTE